Mindfulness For Beginners

100 Essential Meditations to Reduce Your Stress, Anxiety Relief, Overcome Depression: Guided Meditations for Creating Balance & Inner Strength for Improving Mental Health

By

Rafael Kain

© **Copyright 2018 by Rafael Kain**

All rights reserved.

The content contained within this book may not be reproduced, duplicated or transmitted without direct written permission from the author or the publisher.

Under no circumstances will any blame or legal responsibility be held against the publisher, or author, for any damages, reparation, or monetary loss due to the information contained within this book. Either directly or indirectly.

Legal Notice:

This book is copyright protected. This book is only for personal use. You cannot amend, distribute, sell, use, quote or paraphrase any part, or the content within this book, without the consent of the author or publisher.

Disclaimer Notice:

Please note the information contained within this document is for educational and entertainment purposes only. All effort has been executed to present accurate, up to date, and reliable, complete information. No warranties of any kind are declared or implied. Readers acknowledge that the author is not engaging in the rendering of legal, financial, medical or professional advice. The content within this book has been derived from various sources. Please consult a licensed professional before attempting any techniques outlined in this book.

By reading this document, the reader agrees that under no circumstances is the author responsible for any losses, direct or indirect, which are incurred as a result of the use of information contained within this document, including, but not limited to, — errors, omissions, or inaccuracies.

Table of Contents

Introduction 9
Chapter One: What is Stress? 11
   Your Body's Response 12
   Difference between Stress and a Stressor 13
   Different Kinds of Stress 13
   How do You Respond to Stress? 17
   How Much Stress should You Handle 18
Chapter Two: Causes of stress 20
   General Causes 20
   Stressors in Life 22
   Stress at Work 23
   Other Causes of Stress 24
Chapter Three: Effects of Stress on the Body 28
   Central Nervous and Endocrine Systems 29
   Respiratory and Cardiovascular Systems 30
   Digestive System 31
   Sexuality and the Reproductive System 31
   Immune System 32
Chapter Four: Understanding Responses and Signals 33
   Interpreting the Signals of the Central Nervous System 35
   How to Treat the Nervous System 37
Chapter Five: Stress Management 38
   Identify the Stressors in Life 38

Mindfulness for Beginners

Stress Journal 39

Understand How You Cope with Stress 40

Avoid Unnecessary Stress... 42

Alter the Situation 43

Adapt... 45

Accept Things 46

Relax 47

Chapter Six: Natural Ways to Treat Stress........................ 50

Massage 50

Meditation 51

Exercise... 51

Sorting Your Life.. 52

Eat Healthily 52

Limit the Use of Cellphones and the Internet 53

Vitamin B 54

Aromatherapy 54

Sleep 55

Chapter Seven: How to Lead a Stress-Free Life 56

One Task at a Time 56

Have a Simple Schedule 56

Move 57

Develop a Healthy Habit 57

Do Something Calm... 58

Manage Your Finances 58

Have Fun Every Day!... 59

Get Creative 59

Declutter 59

Always be on Time 60

Chapter Eight: Introduction to Meditation 61

Myths about Meditation 63

Chapter Nine: Benefits of Meditation 69

A Calming Effect 69

Stimulates Brain Activity 69

Improves Focus 70

Reduces Stress 70

Reduces Anxiety 71

Promotes Emotional Health 72

Improves Self-Awareness 73

Can Help You be Kind 74

Helps to Control Pain 76

Chapter Ten: Basic Instructions for Meditation 77

The Physical Situation 78

Posture 79

State of Mind 83

Chapter Eleven: Breathing 85

Breathe Comfortably 85

Concentrate on Every Breath 87

Observe Your Breathing and the Sensation 88

Select Your Focus Spot 88

Spread the Awareness throughout Your Body 89

Allow the Breath to Course through You 89

Chapter Twelve: Types of Meditation 91

- General Types of Meditation 91
- Meditation Techniques 93

Chapter Thirteen: How should You Come Out of Meditation? 117

- Reflect on the Meditation 117
- Spread Goodwill and Cheer 118
- Show Sensitivity to Your Breath Energy 118

Chapter Fourteen: What is Mindfulness? 120

- What is Mindfulness? 121
- How to Practice Mindfulness? 123
- Benefits of Mindfulness 124

Chapter Fifteen: Debunking Myths about Mindfulness .. 127

- You Should Only Focus on One Thing 127
- Mindfulness is Not Psychological Therapy 128
- Empty Your Mind if You Want to Meditate 129
- Only if People are Relaxed can They be Mindful 129
- Positivity and Joy Come from You 130
- Changing Your Habits 131
- It Takes Time 131
- You Escape Reality 132
- It is Boring 132

Chapter Sixteen: Mindfulness Exercises 134

- Mindfulness Activities for Group Therapy and Groups 135
- 6 Fun Mindfulness Interventions, Techniques, and Worksheets for Adults 145
- Introducing Dialectical Behavioral Therapy (DBT) 160

5 Simple Mindfulness Exercises from DBT 163
Conclusion 167
Sources 168

Introduction

Do you remember the last time you had a peaceful sleep? Does your mind always worry about everything in your life when you want to sleep or when you want to focus on something? Regardless of what you do, your mind will not stop over-thinking?

When you force yourself to stop thinking about something, the thoughts will flood your brain with renewed strength. You try to tell yourself that there is nothing to worry about, but realize that there are countless things that you can worry about. You change your position, fluff up the pillow and roll over, but you start thinking again. You continue to think until your alarm rings and start getting ready for the day. You try to stay awake throughout the day, but find it difficult to stop yawning. You cannot concentrate throughout the day and don't finish any of the work you have for the day. This leads to undue stress because you worry about what your boss may say to you.

This book will help you find ways to stay content and find peace in such troubled times. Over the course of this book, you will gather information on what stress is and the different reasons why people find themselves under stress. People worry every minute of their life and they want to achieve so much, that they stop living. This book will help you learn the art of being mindful. It is important for us to be mindful to ensure that we enjoy every minute of our lives. This will ensure that we are happy.

If you are constantly worried or anxious about how your life is, you have come to the right place. The exercises mentioned in this book will help you find happiness and stop worrying about your past or future. You should remember that you cannot become mindful when you only practice the exercise once. You should persevere and perform these exercises regularly. This will help you to become mindful and will give you full control of your mind.

Thank you for purchasing this book. I hope it benefits you.

Chapter One: What is Stress?

We often use the word stress to describe our emotions when we experience different emotions that burden us. We find it hard to cope with the pressure and begin to cave into the stress. Our lives are full of frustrations, deadlines and demands. Because of these demands, most of our lives run with stress as the main stimulant. Stress is not bad. In some situations, stress is what makes you react and reach your deadlines. It also motivates you to do your best. Stress becomes bad when you constantly do your work under pressure. This kind of stress affects your mind and your body. You may pay a terrible price because of the effects of stress.

Stress is a regular physical response to events that upset the balance in your life in some way or the other. Your mind sometimes senses danger that could be either real or imaginary. When your mind senses such a type of danger, it stimulates your body into the 'Fight—Flight—Freeze' mode, commonly known as the stress response.

This response is your body's way of protecting you from harm. When this response is functioning correctly, you stay alert, focused and energetic. This response helps you rise to an occasion and helps you face challenges you would not have ever dreamed of completing. To a point, this response also stops being helpful. It has many effects on your body and mind. It invariably affects both your personal and professional lives. The excess of stress deteriorates the quality of life.

Your Body's Response

Your mind always perceives the danger. This danger could either be real or imaginary. When your mind perceives any danger, it sends a signal to your nervous system. The nervous system responds by releasing a rush of stress hormones. These hormones majorly constitute adrenaline and cortisol. It is through these hormones that your body wakes up and realizes that there is an emergency.

When your body understands that it is in danger, it shows many changes. Your muscles tighten, your blood pressure rises, and your senses become extremely sharp. When these physical changes occur, your stamina and strength increase, helping in enhancing your focus. This helps in deciding whether you must fight or flee from the situation at hand.

Difference between Stress and a Stressor

As mentioned above, stress is the emotion or feeling one possesses when they are under pressure. Stressors are those agents that stimulate or cause stress. They are the things in our surrounding environment that cause stress. For example, unpleasant neighbors, speeding cars, or even our relationships, are stressors. People experience more stress when they are exposed to more stressors.

Different Kinds of Stress

Once we realize that we are under stress, we must also identify the intensity of that stress. It helps to know the type of stress, recognize the stressor and the effects it has on you. Psychologists have grouped stress into three categories to provide a better understanding. Through this section, we will understand the different types of stress, their characteristics and symptoms.

Acute Stress

People often experience acute stress. This is usually caused due to the demands and pressures that one faces in their regular lives. The word stress usually gives a negative impression. But it is acute stress that brings joy and excitement in life. For instance, when you are on a water slide, it brings a certain amount of stress. But there is also excitement. This stress is acute stress; however, these rides sometimes bring so much stress, making you wish that the ride ended sooner. Because of this stress, you may feel effects like vomiting, headaches and some other psychological symptoms or physiological symptoms. Since acute stress only occurs for a minute period, the symptoms come out only when you are under stress. The following list provides the common symptoms of acute stress:

- Emotional distress such as irritability and short periods of depression

- Physical distress such as pain, headache, dizziness, nausea and bowel disorders

Episodic Stress

There are times when people are frequently under acute

stress. This type of stress is known as episodic stress. People who make unrealistic demands and set up unreasonable challenges for themselves suffer from episodic stress. When these demands and challenges pile up, they bring too much stress in our attempt to achieve these goals. This type of stress ceases from time to time, though not as frequently as acute stress. People who are competitive suffer from episodic stress. These people belong to the category of "Type A" personality. These people are also aggressive, demanding and are sometimes tense and hostile. The symptoms given below are the most common symptoms found in "Type A" personalities.

- Long periods of depression, anxiety and emotional distress
- Worrying continually
- Heart problems and coronary heart disease

Chronic Stress

Chronic stress is the opposite of acute stress. It does not bring excitement or thrill and is always dangerous and is very unhealthy. It tears the person's life apart and severely affects their mind, body, and spirit.

Long-term exposure to different stressors, such as traumatic experiences, unhealthy relationships, career issues, and dysfunctional families, lead to chronic stress. For the majority of these, the situations seem unending and the accumulated stress leads to problems that are life-threatening. You can develop illnesses like heart diseases, cancer and psychological problems like post-traumatic stress disorder.

The most common symptoms of chronic stress are:

- Parched mouth
- Difficulty in breathing
- Pounding heart
- Headache
- Frequent urination

Some of the mental symptoms of chronic stress are:

- Irritability
- Problems with concentration
- Insomnia
- Feelings of fatigue

How do You Respond to Stress?

You must always remember to recognize the level of stress you are under. You must also identify the kind of stress you are under. The dangerous thing about stress is that you can never identify the intensity of stress you are under. You adapt to this stress and begin to find the feelings and emotions that come with stress as normal. You will only know how bad the situation is when you begin to have physical and mental breakdowns.

The signs of stress overload can be anything. It affects the mind and body intensely and in many ways. It cannot just be overwhelming, but it takes its toll on both your personal and professional relationships.

There are three common ways in which people respond when they are under stress:

- An angry response. It is because of the release of hormones that you find it difficult to sit. You will also be emotional.

- A depressed response. You shut down and have a very little amount of energy. You pull away and space out.

- A tense response. You freeze under pressure because of this response. You feel paralyzed and become very agitated.

How Much Stress should You Handle

Just like how you should always know your limit, you must also know your limit to the amount of stress that you can handle. How much stress a person can handle differs from person to person. Some people like to work with punches while the others like to work with far smaller frustrations. Some people tend to thrive on a highly stressful lifestyle.

Your ability to handle stress depends on multiple factors, including the quality of your relationships and your outlook on life.

Things that affect your tolerance levels are:

- Your family and friends are your enormous buffers against the stressors that you face daily. If you isolate yourself from the people around you, you will be more vulnerable to stress.

- Your sense of confidence and your ability to change events and your ability to overcome challenges says a lot about your tolerance levels. You may sometimes find it difficult to tolerate stress when you find things in your life as being out of control.

- When you are optimistic in life, you tend to overcome stress because of your positivity. If you are pessimistic, you will not accept changes to your life and will find yourself in an immensely stressful situation.

- Your ability to deal with situations is what matters. If you are extremely emotional, you will feel like exploding under pressure. If you are emotionally strong, you will be able to balance the challenges you are facing and decrease the amount of stress you are under.

- If you have knowledge about the situation you are under, you know what to expect and will find it easier to cope with the situation.

Chapter Two: Causes of stress

Stress affects everyone. You need to identify the symptoms to be able to manage them. Based on the above types of stress, you will also be able to categorize the stress that you are under.

General Causes

There are multiple reasons why we, generally, are under stress. Here is a look at some of them.

Threat

When you perceive that you are under threat, your body will believe that it is under stress. These threats could be both personal and social threats. Personal threats can include financial threats, threats related to career, and threats because of family. Social threats include the relationships that you have with people around you. Sometimes this stress worsens when we feel that we have no response to the threat that is affecting us. Because of this, we tend to lose control. Generally, any threat to something that is a necessary aspect of life causes us stress.

Fear

Fear is something that one experiences because of the presence of a threat. This threat further leads to stress. The brain starts imagining multiple outcomes because of this stress, without deciphering the real stress source.

Uncertainty

Because of fear, the brain starts to predict multiple outcomes that may be real or imaginary. This leads to uncertainty. Since we are unable to predict, we feel like we have lost control and may feel threatened. This feeling induces a certain amount of stress within us, which could affect both our mind and body.

Cognitive Dissonance

If there is a significant gap between what you think and what you do, a phenomenon called 'cognitive dissonance' will come into play. For example, you may be a nice person, but believe that you have said something to hurt another person. This may or may not be the case, but you will berate yourself and the guilt will become stress. This phenomenon also occurs when you find it difficult to meet your goals and objectives.

Stressors in Life

There are many stressors in life that always cause stress. These include:

- Death of a family member, friend or your spouse, making you highly emotional and putting you under immense stress.

- You are under immense stress when you have health issues.

- When you face problems with your partner you start finding yourself under pressure.

- Any changes in the family, such as dealing with divorce, marriage or separation, causes high levels of stress.

Stress at Work

The UK's Health and Safety Executive listed the following factors as causes of stress in the workplace:

- The control that we have on how we do our work

- The demands of our jobs

- The support we receive from our superiors

- Our professional relationship

- Our understanding of our roles and responsibilities

- Whether someone consults you or not about change

People are exposed to many other stressors in the workplace. These stressors can be anything, such as your absence at work or the lack of communication within your team. Sometimes the lack of feedback or praise on a task that we have completed can also lead to stress. Other factors include:

- Long hours of work

- No proper training
- No clarity of roles and responsibilities
- Bad ambiance

Other Causes of Stress

If we attempt to ignore stress, it will only end up multiplying and causing more problems. Although it is important to tackle stress, there are some stressors you can ignore.

Reliving Stressful Situations

It is the belief of many experts in the field of stress management that replaying a stressful situation in your mind has nothing but a negative impact. In fact, all it does is for the person to relive that situation and be subject to the same stress all over again. Most experts say that it is easier to just replace that thought rather than try to suppress it.

Having positive thoughts such as, "I am healthy and well" and "I can make it through this and move forward," can really help in avoiding a stress relapse. Also, taking some time out from your life to meditate is also proven to have a very good effect.

Thinking about the Worst Possible Outcomes of a Situation

Thinking about the worst-case scenario of any situation before there is any outcome does not help you either. You begin to imagine only the negative outcomes in any situation, which begins to increase the stress you feel. You can avoid this since you only believe the worst will happen to you. If that scenario does not play out the way you visualized it, you will find yourself under more stress because you worry about why the situation did not turn out a specific way. Avoid thinking about the possible outcomes before anything happens because it does not help you and only adds to your stress.

Procrastination

Procrastination is putting away your work for later. This generally happens when the person is either scared or overwhelmed by the task at hand. Experts feel that procrastination is also a cause for stress, and is a habit that people can work on.

If you break up your task into smaller tasks, the work appears to become simplified and it does not scare you anymore. This way, you can complete each of the smaller tasks thereby completing the full task.

Excess Usage of Social Media

People who use social media for large amounts of time everyday start comparing themselves to others. If they feel inferior as a result, they begin to think low of themselves, which generates stress. Some people go as far as to judge their self-respect based on these social networking sites. For instance, some people worry about why their picture or post did not receive the same number of likes as another picture or post.

Also, oversharing your information and pictures online provides a greater scope for hurting yourself because not everyone online is a nice person. You can avoid this situation by limiting the number of people who can see what you post.

Worrying about Spent Money

Your finances will always be a stress-causing factor for you. The worst part is thinking about the money that you have already spent, and wondering if you should have spent less. You can't turn back time, so there is no point in thinking about it and piling up stress in your mind.

A very effective method of avoiding over-spending your money is to devise a proper financial plan, with accounts for your savings and an analysis of how much you can spend.

Chapter Three: Effects of Stress on the Body

You cannot avoid stress, and there are many negative effects of stress on the body. But, stress can sometimes have a positive effect on you. When you are under stress, your body reacts by increasing the secretion of certain hormones. It also increases your heart rate and hence more oxygen reaches your brain, which enables you to think sharper. In other words, short-term stress is beneficial to you since it helps you work on your tasks faster.

On the other hand, stress on a long-term basis is harmful. Several events can cause stress. A failed marriage, war, violent attacks, natural disasters can all lead to a condition known as post-traumatic stress disorder (PTSD). These kinds of stress have adverse effects on various parts of your body.

Central Nervous and Endocrine Systems

The central nervous system (CNS) controls every activity in the body. The system comprises of the spinal cord and the brain. The endocrine system consists of glands, which secrete hormones that cause a change in the way certain parts of your body function.

In a stressful situation, the hypothalamus of your brain signals to the adrenal gland to secrete adrenaline and cortisol. These hormones increase your heart rate and breathing rate and hence increase the amount of oxygen your brain receives. This helps you to think clearly (fight or flight situations). These reactions take place until the stressor subsides. So, if the stressor continues to exist, it could have a toll on your body.

Chronic stress can have various symptoms such as anxiety, depression, withdrawal and headaches. It can also lead to alcohol and drug abuse.

Respiratory and Cardiovascular Systems

Stress hormones affect your respiratory and cardiovascular systems. When you respond to stress, your brain will indicate to your body that there is very little oxygen. Therefore, you breathe faster which leads to excessive pumping of blood to the core of your body. Stress will make it hard for you to breathe if you suffer from respiratory problems like emphysema and asthma.

Since blood flows to the core of your body, your heart will pump faster. Stress hormones cause your blood vessels to constrict and raise your blood pressure. All these processes helps to deliver oxygen to your brain and heart, leaving you with more strength and energy to act.

Frequent or chronic stress will make your heart work too hard thereby increasing the risk of developing hypertension, heart disease and problems with your blood vessels. You are at higher risk of having a stroke or heart attack. Women in the pre-menopausal stage have a lower risk of developing stress-related heart disease because of the female hormone estrogen.

Digestive System

When you are under stress, your liver starts converting the stored glycogen into glucose to give you an energy boost to react to the stress. When you are in a stressful environment, your body will use all the unused blood sugar. If you are subject to chronic stress, your body may not be able to manage this excess glucose which in turn leads to an increased risk of developing Type 2 diabetes.

This can also influence your digestive system. It can lead to acid reflux and can cause existing ulcers to act up (it does not cause the ulcers to grow). It can also lead to vomiting, diarrhea, and constipation.

Sexuality and the Reproductive System

As mentioned before, stress can have a wide range of effects on both body and mind. This can create fatigue, which decreases the sexual desire of the individual. In the case of short-term stress, the body releases large quantities of the male sex hormone, testosterone. This increases sexual arousal.

When it comes to women, stress affects the menstrual cycle. It could give rise to delayed or no menstruation. If you are under stress during menopause, you will find that the physical symptoms are magnified.

In cases of long-term stress, a man's testosterone level begins to drop. This decreases the sperm count and can also lead to erectile dysfunction or impotence.

Immune System

Stress acts as a stimulus to the immune system. Just like the sexual and reproductive systems, short-term stress can be beneficial to the immune system. The immune system acts up when the person is subject to short-term stress. Long-term stress can increase the susceptibility of the person to infections and diseases and it can also increase their recovery times.

Chapter Four: Understanding Responses and Signals

Before we identify different ways to effectively treat stress, we must identify the signals and understand how the central nervous system functions.

The nervous system (NS) is the link between the body and the environment. It receives information from the environment, interprets it, and tries to find the right response to the stimulus. Modern medicine believes that the nervous system only functions on the physical being and does not work with stimuli in the environment. There are millions of sensory neurons across the body that monitor the reactions to stimuli, and help you build experiences with your external environment. There are also 12 billion cells, maybe more, that constitute the brain. This makes the central nervous system the most important system in the human body. This system helps us to coordinate and integrate with the most important aspects of our lives. If this system is impaired, it diminishes the tone, color, richness, and quality of life.

The central nervous system serves a greater purpose than just being our quarterback. This is the place where we can create, think abstractly, dream, and receive any impressions. This is the connection that we have with the universal consciousness.

Western scientific culture has helped us understand how the human body works and what the different diseases are that affect it. There are some factors that western medicine is still unable to understand and these factors always give rise to new questions.

This continuous exploration has provided us with an understanding of how the human body reacts to its environment. This progress has helped us explore areas of human metabolism that are too subtle for modern medicine to understand. To understand these areas effectively, physiologists, biochemists, microbiologists, physicists, and psychologists must combine their knowledge and expand the boundaries of understanding of the human body. Some physicists of the world now include some aspects of metaphysics and mysticism to their thoughts since they have understood that one cannot understand the whole picture by only looking at tangible, physical parts.

Interpreting the Signals of the Central Nervous System

The nervous system is an interesting aspect of the human body. We can never understand what consciousness is by dissecting the brain. It is difficult to understand how logical and rational thoughts occur and how creative ideas develop in our minds.

It is easy to demonstrate how autonomic nerves control bodily reactions, how the system transmits neurochemicals, parts of the body the neurochemicals target and the parts of the brain that control these processes. But, it is difficult to demonstrate where the awareness has come from and how one understands the necessity to send messages. It is also difficult to understand how one's awareness transmits the needs and desires to the brain to ensure that there is a response to the stimulus.

As human beings, we are not aware of what pain is and why we interpret some impulses as pain or ecstasy. It is difficult to define feelings and emotions and understand where these originate from and the effects that they have on the human body. Why is it that the heart continues to beat until you breathe your last, or why does your breath continue in the same flow without any intervention from your conscience? You should ask these questions if you want to treat stress and anxiety.

Our knowledge of the central nervous system only scratches the surface. There is a point where reasoning and dissection cannot answer some questions. Since most scientists don't look at the theoretical constructs of the higher aspects of the universe, they are unable to answer questions about life, what it is, how it works, and what one's purpose in life is.

You should be more aware of the central nervous system to address both physical and mental wellbeing. Some physicians claim that conventional medicine and treatment is the only way to treat certain disorders. These medicines work with the central nervous system to remove a block or to interpret any signals that are hampering the functioning of the human body. In some circumstances, the physician may suggest that you operate on the body to surgically remove any blocks. You should understand that surgery is an irreversible act, meaning that you should only resort to surgery if every other option has failed.

How to Treat the Nervous System

The ability of the nerves to interpret and react to external stimuli provides feedback to the conscience and the brain about vital aspects of the human body. If you are suffering from any distress or pain, it means that there are imbalances in your body. This is only a signal or a warning to you but is not the cause of the imbalance. If an alarm were to go off in the building you reside in, you will not turn off the alarm but will look for the source. You will try to understand what caused the alarm to ring and identify a solution.

To continue further on the same analogy, it is appropriate to turn off the alarm at times, so you can think straight and identify a plan of action. Conventional medicine works effectively to reduce acute pain. People often forget to identify the cause of the symptom and are happy when the pain subsides.

The approach presented in this book is to use herbs to effectively treat stress and anxiety. You can use a combination of these treatments and conventional medicine to lead a happy life.

Chapter Five: Stress Management

It is true that you cannot avoid stress but you can mitigate its effects. There will always be bills you need to pay, family troubles and other stress-causing events. If you can manage these properly, stress should not build up and affect you. Here are a few tips on how to manage stress.

Identify the Stressors in Life

To be able to manage any issue in life, you will need to begin from the root cause. In a similar way, to manage stress you should identify the stressors. This process is not as easy as it sounds. You may always overlook the actual cause of stress and list the factors that are not the cause. You are worried about the work you have at the office. This worry stems from the fact that you did not begin your work on time. To identify the stressors in your life, you must start understanding your habits and attitude towards work and life in general.

Try identifying how you perceive stress. See if you blame the world for you being under stress. What you must realize is that you need to accept responsibility for feeling under stress. It is usually because of your habits and not because of the world outside.

Stress Journal

A stress journal is the best option for understanding the stressors in your life. It helps you identify the regular stressors. Once you recognize a pattern, you will identify ways to overcome this stress. What you could note down in your stress journal is:

- What element caused stress? It is all right to guess sometimes if you are unsure

- What were your emotions when you felt the stress?

- What was your reaction?

- How did you make yourself feel better?

Understand How You Cope with Stress

Once you have realized that you are under stress and identified the stressor, you should see how you cope with the stress. Your stress journal will help you identify the methods you use to cope with stress. You could have healthy and unhealthy ways of coping with stress. Unfortunately, most people cope with stress in an unhealthy manner, which leads to worsening the physical and mental health of the person.

Unhealthy Ways

Most people, especially the younger generation, adopt these methods to help reduce stress. What they do not realize is that these methods cause an irreparable damage on their systems. Some of the most common ways are:

- Smoking
- Drinking
- Taking pills to reduce stress
- Overeating

- Busying oneself so that we have no time to think or breathe

- Withdrawing from support

- Releasing all the frustration on others

Healthy Ways

When you realize that your methods of managing stress are not actually helping you physically or emotionally, you should look at healthier ways to let off steam and relieve the stress. There are multiple ways to help manage stress in a healthy manner. When you realize that the situation is going to cause stress, try to avoid the situation or change your reaction. When you are trying to figure out what you must do, you could think of the following:

- Avoid

- Adapt

- Alter

- Accept

Avoid Unnecessary Stress

In chapter 3, we have mentioned the unnecessary stress that you must avoid and how you can overcome stress because of the stressors. Here are a few more methods:

Say NO

You should know your limits. One can only stretch so much to achieve a challenge. You must avoid letting additional challenges stick to you. Say no before the challenges stress you out. These challenges could be in both your personal and professional lives.

Avoid People Who are Stressors

If you find that a relationship is always stressing you out and you are not able to turn the relationship around, you can break off ties with the person. This will leave you feeling calmer.

Control Your Environment

If you find stressors in your environment, get rid of them. Do not let them affect you in ways that would give you too much stress.

Prepare Your to-Do List

Analyze your responsibilities. Also, analyze your schedule. Depending on your schedule, you should be able to identify the work you would like to take up and the work that you cannot. Prioritize your list and work downwards.

Alter the Situation

If you find that there is a situation that you cannot handle, you can try to alter the situation. Try to understand what changes you can make so that the problem does not affect you or stress you out in any way. Also, ensure that when you alter the situation, you are not causing problems for yourself in the future.

Express Your Feelings

If there are people bothering you or a situation is bothering you, communicate your feelings and concerns. If you do not voice your opinion, you will feel resentment towards the people and the situation will remain the same. If you let them know how you feel, you will be able to alter the outcome of the situation.

Compromise

You cannot always expect things to go your way. The world does not go by your way or the high way. If you expect someone to change for you, you should also be willing to change for them, if necessary. It is best to stick to the middle ground if you want to relieve yourself of stress. You should remember that compromising does not mean that you are being submissive.

Be Assertive

Take charge of your life. You need to always rise to an occasion and prove your worth. If you need to tell someone something, be confident and say it. Be respectful of the person, but you need to speak your mind.

Adapt

At times, we find it difficult to change the stressor. We will then have to change ourselves. We will need to adapt to stressful situations and regain control over ourselves. You will have to start changing your expectations and attitudes towards a situation that remains the same.

Reframe

Try being optimistic about a problem. When you are pessimistic, you only have negative thoughts, which won't help the situation. Instead of looking at every problem in a negative way, try looking at it in a positive way to help you overcome the situation.

Level Your Standards

Most of us strive to be perfect. This causes an undue amount of stress that sets us up for failure in the future. Always remember to set reasonable standards for yourself and avoid comparing yourself to others.

Look at the Bigger Picture

Always look at the bigger picture. It is all right to fail sometimes. It only helps you learn and move forward!

Accept Things

In some situations, stress is unavoidable. You cannot prevent or change the stressors. The best way to cope with the stress in such a situation is to accept things the way they are. This will be difficult for you to do, but in the long-run it'll help smooth things over.

Look for the Upside

"What doesn't kill us makes us stronger." That is a saying most of us would have come across many a time. When you face major challenges in life, look at them as opportunities to grow both personally and professionally.

Share Your Feelings

Expressing, or communicating, is the best way to remove stress. You'll feel much better and calm. Talk to a trusted friend or meet with a therapist. Tell them how you feel and give them examples of situations where you were under stress. They may help you identify a solution to the problem.

Forgive

Learn to forgive people. Everyone makes mistakes. Nobody is perfect. Let go of your anger and forgive the people who have made the mistake. Remember to forgive yourself when you make a mistake, too.

Relax

You will need to take charge of your life and take charge of nurturing yourself. You need to find time to relax and have fun with family, or alone. When you do this, you will find yourself in a better place in life. It is important to set some time out for yourself and perform activities that you love to do.

Healthy Ways to Relax:

- Walk
- Run
- Drink coffee
- Write in your journal
- Take a long bath
- Listen to music
- Watch comedy
- Workout
- Call a friend

Ensure that you have time for yourself. You should never let the many issues you have cloud your happiness. Your body has needs and you need to cater to them, too.

Set Aside Time

Set aside time for relaxation in your schedule. Do not let

any obligations use up your relaxation time. You need to take a break occasionally from life.

Connect with Others

Spend time with positive people. This will help improve the quality of life for you. You will find that you are able to view your life from a different perspective.

Do the Things You Enjoy

If you like to sleep on the roof and find that it calms you down, you should certainly try it. You do not have to worry about what other people may think since that will only add to your stress.

Chapter Six: Natural Ways to Treat Stress

People are under tremendous stress because they have many things to do and achieve. This stress, when ignored, accumulates and has a negative effect on the human body. Instead of choosing to pop pills when you are anxious, you can use one of the methods in this chapter.

Massage

Everybody loves a massage. I went for my first massage four years ago, and I feel better and happier when I leave the spa or salon. Did you know that massages have been used as a therapy for stress relief for hundreds, maybe even thousands, of years? The Chinese used massage to help them open energy channels to improve their health. It is also said that Hippocrates used friction to treat certain physical ailments. In today's world, massages help to reduce pain, improve circulation, and relax muscles that are stressed or tense. Massage also does wonders to the mind, since a happy body leads to a happy mind.

Meditation

Meditation is an effective way to relieve stress. You do not need to spend more than ten minutes a day to meditate, even when you have a packed schedule. This is a treatment that is affordable since the only tool you will be using is your mind. All you need to do is give yourself some time to focus on your breathing or to let your thoughts run with the wind. This small amount of peace in your day will help you deal with stress and relieve the stress that you feel.

Exercise

Regardless of whether it is running, tai chi, swimming, or yoga, exercise gives you the time to be alone. This will help you understand your thoughts better and may also help you with letting some thoughts go. Unlike meditation, exercise not only gives you a sense of calm but also releases endorphins in your brain, which improve your mood. This method helps to prevent obesity and related health disorders giving you a little less to worry about.

Sorting Your Life

When you organize and sort your life, you will be able to obtain a sense of calm. When you organize your life, you will be able to build a sense of control that will help you improve the way you function. If you are someone who leads a fast life, it would be a good idea to make a "to-do" list that will help you remember all the tasks that you would need to complete. If you find that a clumsy house causes distress, clean the house. Studies have concluded that for some, the sight of clutter puts them on edge.

Eat Healthily

Studies have concluded that junk food does indeed make one depressed. It is essential that you start substituting junk food with fruits, vegetables, grains, and nuts. It is always good to swap junk food with healthy food like protein and whole grains, since they help to improve your mood and give you the energy to tackle any task or hurdle that comes your way. According to some scientists, almonds, salmon, and blueberries are known to be kickass stress busters.

Reduce your coffee intake to one cup a day. Many studies have shown that coffee during the day does offer benefits, but it is important to remember that too much caffeine induces anxiety and may lead to a dip in the quality of your life.

Limit the Use of Cellphones and the Internet

Have you been to a city or a country when you were unable to maintain contact with the outside world? If you have been in this situation, how did you feel? Did you find that disconnecting from the world did indeed have a good effect on your mental wellbeing?

One reason behind why it is difficult to relieve stress in today's world is that we are unable to shield ourselves from it. If you were to turn off the internet or switch your mobile phone off, you would be blocking some channels that cause you stress. This will help you to live in the moment and appreciate every second of it.

It is important to switch off all electronics before you sleep. It is better to avoid using any electronics before you sleep to reduce the problem of insomnia.

Vitamin B

Vitamin B is known to improve the functioning of the nervous system and the brain. It is also good for fighting fatigue and inducing relaxation. Some symptoms of Vitamin B deficiency include apathy, depression, and irritability. If you want to avoid these symptoms, it is best to add vitamin B-rich foods to your diet. Beans, nuts, peas, eggs, dairy products, liver, and bran and germ cereal grains are the best sources of vitamin B.

Aromatherapy

Studies have shown that inhaling some scents have an immediate effect on the body and help to relieve stress and anxiety. These scents also help with improving concentration and focus. Experts suggest that this occurs since smells act as a stimulus to the limbic system. This system releases chemicals in the brain that promote the feeling of love, excitement, calmness, and relaxation. Some oils used in aromatherapy are cypress, rosemary, and lavender.

Sleep

This is one of the most important methods of relieving stress. If you have very little sleep, you are bound to be irritable, cranky, and possibly on edge throughout the day. If you oversleep, you will be sluggish, lazy, and depressed. Always strike a balance to ensure that you feel well rested throughout the day. You must ensure that you sleep at a proper time. All you will need to do is signal to the brain that you will need to sleep at a time and wake up the following morning at a time. Some foods like bananas, carbohydrates, figs, peanuts, and dairy promote sleep. These foods are effective since they contain tryptophans – a compound that contains melatonin. Ensure that you do not eat a heavy meal right before bed since this could lead to reflux, heartburn, or indigestion.

Chapter Seven: How to Lead a Stress-Free Life

We have looked at different ways you can relieve stress and anxiety. This chapter focuses on how you can change your lifestyle to lead a stress-free life.

One Task at a Time

This is the easiest way to begin your journey, and you can start this right away. Focus on working on one task at a time to ensure that you do not burden yourself with all tasks at once. Remove any distractions you may have from your desk and pick one task to work on. You should practice this continuously to ensure that you become better.

Have a Simple Schedule

When you have a hectic schedule, you will lead a stressful life. It is best to reduce the number of commitments you have in life to make sure that you do justice to the essential ones. Always learn to say no to those commitments that are not worth your time and get out of negative commitments. Schedule your day in a way that allows you to breathe and have some time for yourself.

Move

It is important that you are always active – walk, play a sport, dance, do yoga, go for a run, hike. The task does not have to be grueling, but you should have fun doing it.

Develop a Healthy Habit

It is important to improve your health to reduce stress. Begin to eat healthily and try to cultivate a habit each month. You can start by eating healthily, quitting drinking or smoking, drinking a lot of water, or forming a habit that is healthy for you.

Do Something Calm

Always perform activities that calm you. For some people, an activity that gets them moving keeps them calm. But, there are activities like taking a bath, napping, writing, reading or watching a movie that will help you stay calm. Try to find an activity that calms you down and perform it each day.

Manage Your Finances

Finances can cause a lot of undue stress, and if that is the case with you, you must find a way to simplify things. It is always better to automate bill payments, debt payments, and savings. Try spending less time shopping online and eating out. You must try to identify ways that do not involve you spending your money.

Have Fun Every Day!

It is important that you have fun every day, even if you only have fun for a few minutes. Try to take some time off and perform an activity or exercise that will make you laugh your heart out.

Get Creative

It is always good to throw yourself into a creative activity that will keep your mind occupied. You can write, paint, sketch, or sing if you like any of those activities. Or, you can choose an activity that brings out your creativity.

Declutter

This is a favorite activity for most people. You can just go through your stuff and remove things that you do not need anymore or do not use. Then, look around your house and remove things that you do not need or use any longer. This way you will be able to create a calm environment to live in. You can do this a little at a time to ensure that you do not lose out on too many things.

Always be on Time

When you are late, you will want to complete all your tasks in a short period of time since you would not want to stay longer to finish your tasks. This leads to undue stress. It is best to leave early or get ready early so you have enough time to complete all your tasks. It is okay to be early since that will give you some time to prepare or a long time to rest between breaks.

Chapter Eight: Introduction to Meditation

Most people believe that meditation is synonymous to breathing in yoga. But, meditation is more than that. Through meditation, you can learn to focus. You can train your mind and rewire the electrical circuits to ensure that you develop skills and strengths that you require to solve problems. There are different types of meditation that you can follow to help you achieve your goals. The different types of meditation are covered later in the book.

The techniques mentioned and taught in this book will help you reduce stress. These techniques will help you focus on the present and not on the emotions or thoughts that drive you. You will also learn to control some reactions to stress. You must remember that the stress that you face is limiting your happiness. You are often stressed because you believe that you are not happy with where you are in your life. There are many people who constantly work because they want to amass enough wealth to support their family. But, do you think they lead a happy life? Do you think they spend time with their kids? The answer to both these questions is no. They only believe they are happy.

If you lead such a life, you should practice meditation

since it will help you identify your priorities. You can uncover the mysteries of your mind and see why your mind does what it does to help you stay happy. You will also understand how to overcome such efforts. Only when you identify this will you be able to attain genuine happiness. This is the happiness that never lets you down and never changes. You can be confident that this happiness will last for a very long time.

Through meditation, you will learn that you can genuinely be happy. You will learn that you do not have to resort to temporary happiness. You will learn to train your mind to find happiness within yourself and not in an outside person or power.

The goal of meditation is to remove stress and to keep you happy. You will develop qualities like honesty, compassion, integrity, and mindfulness, and will learn that happiness comes from within you. It does not require the affirmation of another person. Meditation is hence a practice that helps in spreading happiness and kindness within you and within people around you.

When you begin to meditate, you learn how to de-stress. When you are calm, you will learn to maintain your temper and will stop depending on people to help you solve your problems. When you are under stress, you place an extra burden on yourself and on the people around you, which affects your relationships. But when your mind learns how to stop causing stress, you will find yourself in a position where you can help yourself and others. Hence, through the practice of meditation, you will learn to respect yourself for the things that you are worthy of. You will find that your desire to gain happiness does not harm you or the society around you. You will be able to find happiness for yourself on your own.

Myths about Meditation

Meditation is only about Concentration

Meditation is not concentration. When you meditate, you learn to focus better on the tasks at hand. Unlike concentration, meditation is a relaxation technique and does not require any effort. You learn to let go of your emotions and thoughts and find yourself in a state of deep relaxation. It is, therefore, easier for you to concentrate.

Meditation is a Religious Practice

Meditation and yoga transcend every religion since they are ancient practices. There is no criterion as to which religion can meditate and which cannot. Meditation can probably bring faiths, nations and countries together. Meditation benefits every human being on the planet. 'Gurudev' Sri Sri Ravi Shankar once said that he would like to encourage people from all backgrounds to meditate.

Always Sit in the Lotus Posture When You Meditate

A scientific study called the 'Patanjali Yoga Sutras' unravels the nature of the human mind. The study says that people must be steady and comfortable when they meditate since it enhances their experience. You can either sit cross-legged on a chair or sofa. You can also stand if that makes you feel better. You only need to ensure that your back is straight.

Only Old People should Meditate

Meditation adds value to people of any age group. You can start meditating at the age of ten. Meditation is synonymous to a shower, in the sense that it helps to keep your mind stress-free and clear, just how a shower keeps your body clean.

Meditation is like Hypnotism

Meditation is a medicine for hypnosis. When a person is hypnotized, he or she is not aware of what they are doing. Meditation is about being aware of every moment in your life. While hypnotism makes a person believe in the impressions in their mind, meditation helps to free the person from those impressions. It helps to clear their consciousness. While hypnotism increases metabolic activity, meditation decreases it.

Meditation Controls Your Thoughts

People do not invite their thoughts. They are aware of their thoughts only when they pass through your mind. A thought is like the clouds in the sky: they come when they want to and go away on their own. If you want to control your thoughts, you must make extra effort. When you meditate, you do not allow your mind to dwell on the positive thoughts or reject the negative thoughts. You only witness your thoughts and move them into a silent space within your mind.

Meditation Helps You Run Away from Problems

Meditation helps to empower people to face their problems with a smile. Through meditation, one can develop the skills to handle any situation in a constructive and pleasant manner. You can learn to accept a situation for what it is and then make a conscious effort to work on that situation. You will stop worrying about the future and forget the past. When you meditate regularly, you will find that you have better self-esteem and have the strength to take up new challenges. Meditation will help you move ahead in life with confidence.

You Must Meditate for Hours to Experience Bliss

People do not have to sit down for hours to enhance their experience. You can establish a connection with your source in a fraction of a second. If you meditate for at least twenty minutes each and every day, you will develop a strong connection with your inner self. The quality of your meditation will also improve and you will experience the benefits of meditation.

You will become a Recluse or a Monk if You Meditate

It is not necessary for one to give up their material life if they want to lead a spiritual life. When you meditate, the quality of your life improves and you learn to appreciate the little things in life. You can be happy and keep the people around you happy when you have a peaceful and relaxed mind.

You should Face Certain Directions and only Meditate at Certain Times

You can meditate whenever you want to and face any direction when you want to meditate. You should keep in mind that your stomach should not be full. Otherwise, you will doze off immediately. It is a good practice to meditate either at sunrise or sunset since it can help to keep you energetic and calm throughout the day.

I hope this chapter has helped to remove your inhibitions about meditation. Now that you have a better idea of what meditation truly is, let us look at the benefits of meditation.

Chapter Nine: Benefits of Meditation

Meditation is an activity that helps to increase your productivity, which leads to happiness. You may wonder how breathing increases productivity. This chapter covers some of the well-known benefits of meditation. When you meditate regularly, you will notice these changes in your body.

A Calming Effect

When you meditate, you try to clear your mind and avoid thinking about anything positive or negative. Studies show that meditation helps to decrease the electrical activity that takes place in the brain, thereby reducing your thoughts. Some studies have compared the electrical activity in the brain of meditators to that of those who don't practice meditation. These studies concluded that people practicing meditation had more gray matter.

Stimulates Brain Activity

Meditation increases the volume of blood flowing into your brain. As mentioned earlier, meditation reduces the electrical activity in your brain. When you meditate, your brain rewires its circuits, which increases the gray matter in your brain. Since meditation helps to rewire the circuits in the brain, it slows the process of aging down for your brain.

Improves Focus

Through meditation, you can focus better on your life. You will learn how to control your thoughts and actions and will stop procrastinating. You will learn to focus more on the task at hand and complete it within a short period. Studies show that students who meditate regularly score well in their exams.

Reduces Stress

Most people are under stress at work, in school or generally in life. They practice meditation or try to meditate to reduce stress. Many studies concluded that meditation does help to reduce stress. Mental and physical stress increases the levels of cortisol, the stress hormone, in the body. This increase of cortisol leads to the release of some chemicals like cytokines, which promote inflammation. The effects of stress can cause insomnia, anxiety and depression, fatigue, lack of focus and an increase in blood pressure.

An eight-week study conducted on mindfulness meditation used 1,300 adults as subjects. This study tested the hypothesis that mindfulness meditation helped to reduce the stress-induced inflammation. Further research shows that meditation also reduces other symptoms of stress, including post-traumatic stress disorder, fibromyalgia and irritable bowel syndrome.

Reduces Anxiety

When you are less stressed, you will be less anxious. In the study mentioned earlier, subjects who practiced mindfulness meditation were less anxious. The study confirmed that meditation helps to reduce anxiety disorders such as social anxiety, phobias, obsessive-compulsive behaviors, panic attacks, and paranoid thoughts.

Three years after the eight-week study, another study conducted used 18 volunteers as subjects. These volunteers practiced meditation regularly and were less anxious when compared to who they were three years ago.

A larger study conducted with 2,466 subjects concluded that different types of meditation had different effects on the body. For instance, yoga is known to help people with anxiety. This can be due to the benefits that the person receives from both physical activity and meditative practice.

Through meditation, you can also control job-related stress and anxiety when you work in high-pressure environments. A study conducted on a group of nurses showed that meditation helped to reduce stress and anxiety.

Promotes Emotional Health

Some types of meditation also help you have a positive approach and outlook on life, and can lead to improved self-image. Studies conducted on mindfulness meditation concluded that depression reduces when one practices meditation. A study conducted on 18 volunteers who practiced meditation for 3 years were less depressed when compared to those who did not practice meditation. As mentioned earlier, stress leads to the release of chemicals called cytokines, and these chemicals lead to depression. Several studies concluded that meditation reduces the release of these chemicals, thereby reducing depression.

Improves Self-Awareness

Some types of meditation help people develop a stronger foundation. They understand themselves better and grow into being the best versions of themselves. For instance, self-inquiry meditation aims to help you develop an understanding of who you are and how you relate to your surroundings. Other types teach you to identify the negative thoughts and learn to control those thoughts. The idea behind these forms is that you make yourself aware of your thoughts and habits, and steer any negative thoughts and habits into constructive patterns. 21 women, who were fighting breast cancer, were subjects in a study. They took part in a tai chi program, and by the end of the program they had better self-esteem when compared to those who only received social support.

Another study conducted on 40 senior women and men

studied their reactions to mindfulness meditation. The study concluded that these senior citizens experienced reduced emotions and feelings of abandonment and loneliness when compared to those who were not a part of the program.

Can Help You be Kind

Some types of meditation increase the positive actions and thoughts towards yourself and others. Metta, often called the 'loving-kindness' meditation, helps you develop kind feelings and thoughts towards yourself. If you continue to practice this type of meditation, you will learn to extend these kind thoughts externally, first to your family and friends, and then to your acquaintances. Multiple studies concluded that this type of meditation helps to increase a person's compassion towards himself and towards the beings around them.

A study conducted on 100 adults shows that when people put more effort into Metta meditation, they experience more positive feelings. Further studies showed that people develop positive feelings through Metta meditation, and these feelings can reduce conflict, help with anger management and reduce social anxiety. When you practice Metta meditation, these feelings accumulate over time.

Rafael Kain

Helps to Control Pain

Your mind controls the way you perceive pain. If you are under stress, this pain will elevate. For instance, a study observed the brain activity of participants when they experienced painful stimuli. Some of the participants practiced mindfulness meditation for four days prior to the study. Patients who meditated before the study showed an increase in the activity in the parts of the brain that help to control pain. These patients also responded less to painful stimuli.

A larger study with 3,500 subjects studied how habitual meditation affected them. This study concluded that meditation reduced the feeling of intermittent and chronic pain. Another study concluded that meditation helped people with terminal diseases manage and mitigate any chronic pain they may feel at the end of life. In these studies, the non-meditators and meditators were under the same pain, but the latter group of people were able to cope better with pain and experienced a reduced feeling of pain.

Chapter Ten: Basic Instructions for Meditation

Meditation does not follow a strict pattern. You can be in any situation or in any position to meditate; however, there are certain postures you should maintain to reap the benefits of meditation. As mentioned earlier, it is best to meditate at sunrise or sunset. You must find a place where you will not be disturbed, either physically or mentally.

Some postures are more favorable when compared to others. For instance, most teachers tell their students to either sit in the lotus or half-lotus position. But, a person can choose to sit cross-legged, stand, lie down or walk when he or she wants to meditate. The only thing you must remember is to keep your back straight.

It is true that meditation is all about the breath, but it is important for you to focus on the physical situation, posture and the state of your mind before you worry about breathing.

The Physical Situation

This section focuses on three main aspects – where you must meditate, when you must meditate and how you must minimize the disturbances.

Where to Meditate

This is a simple one. You will have to choose a quiet place, either at home or outside. If you are going to meditate daily, find yourself a spot where you will not have to perform any other activity. You will create an association with the spot. To ensure that you create a calming effect at that spot, keep it spotlessly clean.

When to Meditate

The best times to meditate are early in the morning or after you have rested from your daily work. Early in the morning, your mind is free from the worries of the day and your body is perfectly rested. It is not good if you meditate right before you sleep since you will begin to associate meditation with sleep. But if you have difficulty sleeping, you can meditate before you sleep since you will be able to fall asleep right after meditating. You must never meditate after eating food since it will only make you drowsy.

Minimize Disturbances

You may be living alone or living with other people. If you are living alone, you will have no problem with ensuring that there is no disturbance around you. If you are living with other people, you will have to tell them that you are working on reducing the amount of stress you are under. Also, mention to them that you are working on becoming a person who is easier to live with. If there are children in your house, you can identify a time when your children have gone to sleep; you can meditate then. Remember to turn all your electronic gadgets off; you should avoid any disturbances. You can have a setting on your mobile whereby you will only obtain a notification if the same person has tried to contact you more than once.

Posture

Before you begin to work on your posture, you will have to work on staying still. It is difficult to stay still for a long time. It is even more difficult to ensure that your mind is calm and without any deviating thoughts.

Sitting on the Floor

The ideal posture that most people follow is sitting on the floor. People usually have a blanket beneath them. This is the perfect posture for meditation for the following reasons:

- You are in a stable position. You will not fall over or hurt yourself. Your mind will be more aware when you progress through the different levels of meditation.

- If you find that this posture is the best for you, you can meditate anywhere you choose to. If you love nature, go to the park, spread a blanket on the ground, and sit. Close your eyes and begin to pay attention to your breath.

Standard Posture

To sit in the standard version, follow the steps given below:

Step 1: You can either sit on the floor or sit on a blanket.

Place your left leg folded on the floor in front of you and place your right leg on top of your left leg. This is known as the 'ardha padmasana.' Then place your hands in your lap, with your palms facing upward. Place your right palm on top of your left palm.

Alternate Position: You can sit in the 'Padmasana' if you choose to. But, first get used to the 'ardha padmasana' pose. Place your left leg folded on the floor in front of you and place your right leg on top of your left leg and then shift your left leg over your right leg. This is the 'padmasana' pose.

Step 2: Move your hands closer to your stomach to keep your back straight.

Step 3: Close your eyes and try focusing on your third eye. If closing your eyes makes you drowsy, you can leave them half open. Find an object to focus on. Ensure that you do not glare at the object but only look at it.

Step 4: Maintain your posture. You must not let your body sway to either the left or the right. If you find that your body is swaying, relax those muscles and make sure that your body shifts back to its original state.

Step 5: Now work on relaxing your muscles. Pull your shoulders down towards your back to create an arch between your middle and lower back. Then, pull your stomach in to ensure that your spine is not the only thing that is keeping your body erect.

Step 6: Now, work on relaxing all the muscles in your body. It is important that you perform this step since it helps in reducing the stress and the strain that your body and mind feel.

Sitting on Benches or Chairs

You may have an illness or an injury that does not allow you to sit on the floor or on a blanket with ease. To avoid this, you can buy yourself a meditation bench; you will have to sit down on your knees and then place the bench next to your back and move up onto the bench. Benches are made at a certain angle and you can buy the one that suits you. There are other benches that allow you to move forward or backward. Most people consider this unstable. Buy a bench that is suitable to your needs.

At times these benches can also prove to be a nuisance. At such times, you can always work on meditating on a chair. Find a chair that is not too high. You will have to be able to touch the ground. The rest of the steps are the same as mentioned above, only you will not sit in either the ardha padmasana or the padmasana pose.

State of Mind

When you sit down in a comfortable position, you should first identify what state your mind is in. Take a few deep breaths and try to assess your mind. Is your mind thinking at the same pace as your breath? Is it thinking of certain events that are making you uncomfortable? If it is the former, then continue to breathe and close your eyes. If you find that some parts of your mind are not cooperating with you, you must use different techniques to counteract them.

You must remember that you must never let your mood decide whether you are going to meditate or not. You must ensure that you do not have a bad meditation session since it amounts to absolutely nothing. You will have to, at the very least, learn how to rid your mind of the unnecessary thoughts that hinder your meditation. Only when you resist these thoughts will you understand them.

If you find that there are certain thoughts that are coming your way, you will have to identify certain methods to rid your mind of those thoughts. These methods will

Rafael Kain

help you remove any negative thoughts, and you can look at things from a different perspective. You will learn to link your thoughts to your breath and calm yourself down.

Chapter Eleven: Breathing

This is the most important part of meditation. Only when you can breathe correctly will you be able to identify your true happiness. There are six simple steps that you must follow to ensure that you are breathing correctly while meditating.

Breathe Comfortably

Begin by taking deep breaths. Through these breaths, you are spreading energy throughout your body. You will be able to observe each breath that you take or release during meditation. It is always a good idea to take in deep breaths at the beginning of meditation since it helps in removing any negative thoughts that you may have while trying to empty your mind.

Initially, notice if there is a difference in your body when you are breathing. You must see if you are able to feel comfortable when you are taking a breath in or releasing it. Notice whether you are comfortable. If you find that you are not comfortable, use the following steps to ensure you are:

Rafael Kain

- Identify the parts of your body that are uncomfortable with the deep breaths. See if you can focus on them and make them comfortable as well.

- Try using different patterns of breathing. That way, it would not be monotonous and you would have a different breath to try every time you find your body uncomfortable.

- Ask yourself what type of breath you would want.

Concentrate on Every Breath

When you start out with meditation, your mind will wander listlessly. Stop wandering and start focusing on your breathing. Your mind will wander again; bring it back to focus on your breathing. This may happen 100 times; it can also happen 1,000 times. Keep bringing it back to focus on your breathing. Do not let yourself down. It takes time to control your mind. To ensure that you focus right from the beginning, you can use a meditation word. You can split the word into two – the first half for when you breathe in and the second for when you breathe out.

Observe Your Breathing and the Sensation

Start observing how different parts of your body feel when you are breathing. First concentrate on your navel. Watch how your belly moves in and out when you are taking deep breaths. See how the navel and the area around the navel feel when you are taking deep breaths. If there are areas that are sensitive to your breathing, identify what type of breathing suits it. Continue this with the rest of your torso.

Initially, you can spend a few minutes with each part of your torso. Once you have mastered the technique of breathing, you can spend an extra amount of time on the different parts during your forthcoming sessions.

Select Your Focus Spot

People ask you to focus on your third eye when you meditate, since the energy in that region is free. When you are meditating, you must focus on a certain part of your body – tip of your nose, your mouth, your eyes, your throat or your breastbone. Instead of worrying about which part to focus on, you can experiment with these body parts during the different meditation sessions and pick the one that is giving you the best results!

Spread the Awareness throughout Your Body

Have you seen how bright a lantern is? Place the lantern in the center of a dark room. You will see that the light has spread to every corner of the room. You must spread the awareness of the breath throughout your body from your focus spot. You will have to tell yourself that it is not just the focus spot that is breathing, but it is your entire body.

Allow the Breath to Course through You

When you are breathing, you must think of all the energy that is associated with the breath. You will find that there is a harmony between the breath and the energy in your body. You must focus only on the breathing. Your body will change the way you breathe depending on the energy in the body. You need not worry about that. Let the energy flow as required throughout your body. You must only focus on the awareness that your body has of breathing and the energy associated with it.

Chapter Twelve: Types of Meditation

The previous chapter covered some of the benefits of meditation. Since there are many people practicing meditation, you may be curious and probably look for information in a bookstore or online. There are different types of meditation techniques, and it may be difficult to identify which type is the best for you. This chapter covers the different types of meditation, briefly explains each of them and helps you understand if the technique is for you. It is important to remember that there is no best type of meditation.

General Types of Meditation

Scientists often categorize meditation into focused attention and open monitoring; however, there is a third type of meditation called effortless presence. Here is a quick look at all three types of meditation practices.

Focused Attention Meditation

In this type of meditation, you should focus only on one object during the full session. The object can be a mantra, visualization, your breath, an external object, a part of your body, etc. When you advance, your ability to focus only on the chosen object becomes stronger. This is because distractions are both short-lived and less common. Both the steadiness and the depth of your attention develop.

Some types of focused attention meditation are Buddhist meditation, chakra meditation, metta meditation, some forms of zazen, and many others.

Open Monitoring Meditation

In this type of meditation, you do not focus only on one object, but monitor all aspects of your experience without any attachment or judgment. You learn to recognize your internal and external perceptions and see them for what they are. This process helps you monitor your thoughts and responses to your surroundings and learn from their experiences without worrying about the negative parts of the experience. Some examples of this type of meditation are: vipassana, some types of Taoist meditation, and mindfulness meditation.

Effortless Presence

This type of meditation is where you do not have to focus on anything. Your attention remains steady, quiet, introverted and empty. This type of meditation is known as "pure being" or "choiceless awareness." Most quotes on meditation only speak about this state. This is the true purpose behind every type of meditation, and therefore is not necessarily a type of meditation. Every traditional technique of meditation recognizes that the process of monitoring thoughts and emotions and the object of focus are a means to train the mind. This practice helps you identify the deeper and inner states of consciousness. Eventually, you are left with the process and the object of focus. Only the true self of the individual is left behind, which is known as the pure presence. There are some techniques of meditation that focus only on this aspect from the beginning.

Meditation Techniques

Zazen (Zen Meditation)

Zazen is a type of seated meditation and has its roots in

the Ch'an tradition that is a type of Chinese zen Buddhism. The popular forms of this type of meditation in the West come from the founder of the Soto Zen movement in Japan, Dogen Zenji. Other types of zazen are practiced in Korea and Japan in the Rinzai School of Zen.

In this form of meditation, you sit on the floor over a cushion or mat and cross your legs. It was traditionally done in the half-lotus or lotus position, but this is not necessary. You must keep your back straight, right from the neck to the pelvic region. Close your mouth and lower your eyes. Your gaze should rest on the ground, maybe three feet in front of you.

The mental aspect of this meditation is practiced in two ways:

Focusing on the breath

You must focus all your attention on the flow of air through your nostrils. You can count the breath in your mind, where you start with number one when you inhale. Continue to count the breaths until you reach the number ten. Resume your count from number one again. If your thoughts and emotions distract you, bring your attention back to your breath and count from number one.

Just sitting or shikantaza

In this form, you do not have to use any specific object to

concentrate. Instead, you must live in the present moment and be aware of your surroundings and your thoughts. You should avoid dwelling on a specific thought. This is a type of effortless meditation.

Zazen is a sober style of meditation and there are many communities that practice this type. There is also plenty of information available for you on the internet. This type of meditation places a lot of emphasis on your posture since that aids your concentration.

Some people also couple other Buddhist elements when they meditate. They may either chant, have group readings or prostrations. There are some people who may like this and there are those who do not. These elements enhance your focus and process.

Vipassana Meditation

Vipassana means "clear seeing" or "insight." This is a traditional Buddhist practice that dates back to 6th century, BC. The Vipassana Movement and S.N. Goenka popularized this type of meditation. Since this type of meditation focuses solely on the breath, it gained popularity in the West and is commonly known as "mindfulness."

Most teachers believe that students must first be mindful of their breath. They will then need to stabilize the mind and concentrate on the breath. This type of meditation is like the focused attention style of meditation. Once the student can focus on the mental phenomena and bodily sensations, the teachers expect the student to develop clear insight. In this state, the student should observe every moment, but not cling to a specific moment.

Sit down on the floor or on a cushion, cross your legs and keep your back erect. You can use a chair, but ensure that you do not support your back against the chair. You should first develop concentration through the practice of samatha, whereby you should focus only on your breath. Focus all your attention on your breath and how it flows through your body. You can also notice the subtle movements in your body, like the movement of the abdomen. You can also focus on how the air feels when it passes through your nostrils. This is a more advanced step and will require a lot of practice.

When you focus on your breath, you will notice that every other sensation and perception continues to occur. You should only acknowledge these moments and then return to your breathing. You should always pay attention to your breath, while every other emotion or thought is only in the background.

Your breathing is the primary object while your thoughts and emotions are the secondary objects. If you notice that a secondary object is diverting your attention, you should focus on that object only for a moment and give it a label. This method is known as noting.

When you give any object a label, you identify that object only by the label and do not worry about the details. When you hear sounds, you should try to label the object as "hearing."

When you gain this concentration, you can turn your attention to the primary object that is either a bodily sensation or a thought. You should observe the object without lettings any thoughts or emotions passing through your mind of their own accord. You can use mental labeling to prevent your mind from chasing a specific thought. Mental labeling will help you notice your thoughts and be objective about them.

It is because of this type of meditation that one can develop the habit of seeing clearly. This sense is pervaded by the marks of existence – the emptiness of the self (annata), dissatisfaction (dukkha) and impermanence (annica). You can develop inner freedom, peace and equanimity through this practice.

This type of meditation is an excellent way to ground

your body and understand how your mind works. It is a popular meditation technique and there are plenty of teachers, schools, books and websites that help you through the process. The teaching is free, therefore there are no formalities attached to this meditation.

If you are new to meditation, you can either start with mindfulness or vipassana meditation techniques.

Mindfulness Meditation

Mindfulness meditation uses the techniques of traditional Buddhist meditation practices but also has strong influences from other types of meditation. The Buddhist term "sati" is where the word mindfulness originated from. Anapanasati, called "the mindfulness of breathing," is a part of insight meditation or vipassana and zazen. John Kabat-Zinn influenced the West to follow the practice of mindfulness. He developed the mindfulness-based stress reduction program (MBSR) in 1979 at the University Of Massachusetts Medical School. This therapy has been used in numerous health clinics and several hospitals over the last few decades.

Mindfulness meditation is a practice where you should focus on the present moment and pay attention to your thoughts, emotions and sensations, without being judgmental.

When you formally practice mindfulness meditation, sit down on the floor or on a cushion and keep your back straight. Close your eyes and pay attention to the movement of your breath. When you take a deep breath, focus only on the breath entering your body. You should try to focus on how you felt when you breathed in. When you exhale, be aware of the air leaving your body. You can perform this exercise repeatedly and ensure that you focus only on your breath. You can also make note of how you feel when you inhale and exhale. Watch your thoughts, feelings and emotions closely. You should not add anything new to the moment, but only be aware of how you feel. You should control your mind and not allow it to chase a specific thought or emotion.

Your mind will wander when a new thought creeps in or when it hears a new sound. If this happens, you should recognize that your mind is chasing a specific thought and bring your attention back to your breathing. The objective is to only acknowledge a sensation or thought. There is a significant difference between being aware of the presence of a sensation or thought and being inside it. You must learn to enjoy the sessions and appreciate how your mind and body feel after the exercise.

You can also practice mindfulness when you perform your regular activities such as talking, eating and walking. The practice is to pay attention to what is happening in the present and be fully aware of the moment. You should not just live automatically. When you talk to someone, you must be aware of the words you are saying, how you are saying them and pay attention to what the other person says.

Loving Kindness Meditation

Loving kindness meditation, also known as the metta meditation, gives you the chance to develop a loving and kind attitude towards everything, including your enemies and the sources of stress. To perform this type of meditation, you must find a quiet space. You can either sit down on the floor or sit on a chair. If you sit on a chair, place your feet firmly on the ground. Take deep breaths and pay attention only to your breath because that is the primary object. Now, send kind and loving messages to the world. You can enhance the effects of this meditation process by sending messages to specific people. The key is to repeat a message multiple times until you feel a sense of love and kindness towards that person.

This type of meditation promotes feelings of love and

compassion for others and for yourself. If you are affected by stress, this type of mediation will help you by:

- Relieving anger and frustration
- Removing resentment
- Clarifying any interpersonal conflict

Through this type of meditation, you can increase your positive emotions. Studies conclude that the loving kindness meditation helps to reduce anxiety, depression and PTSD, or Post Traumatic Stress Disorder.

Breathe Awareness Meditation

Through this type of meditation, you will learn to be mindful of your breath. You should breathe slowly and deeply and count your breaths. This will help you focus on your breath and ignore any other thoughts that enter your mind. The breathe awareness meditation is similar to the mindfulness meditation and offers most of the same benefits, including improved concentration, reduced anxiety, and greater emotional flexibility.

Spiritual Meditation

This type of meditation is used in the Christian faith and in the eastern religions such as Daoism and Hinduism. In spiritual meditation, you focus on the silence around you and try to establish a stronger connection with the universe or God. Essential oils such as frankincense, sage, myrrh, sandalwood, and cedar are used to enhance the experience.

You can practice spiritual meditation either in your place of worship or at home. If you want to grow spiritually, you should practice this type of meditation.

There are different types of spiritual meditation:

Basic Breathing Spiritual Meditation

This is a simple meditation technique and is extremely powerful. When you bring your attention to your breath, you forget about the world out there and only focus on yourself. Your mind will gradually settle and calm down. When the surface part of your mind begins to settle, it will reveal your subconscious, which is known as "pure awareness."

You must remember that when you pay attention to your thoughts, you also show yourself that you love yourself. When you watch your breath, you open the door where you experience deep consciousness. This consciousness facilitates healing.

When you don't try to change your breath, you accept yourself and also allow yourself to be who you are. When you witness yourself in this way, you become your companion. When you stay with this meditation technique, your mind will slow down and you begin to experience love. You will learn to love peace and stillness. When you continue to perform this type of meditation, you will learn who you are.

Present Moment Focus Meditation

Before you begin this meditation, you should tell yourself that there is no past or future. Your ego created this illusion of time to divert your attention from the present. Why will your ego do this to you? If you focus only on the present, there is no grudge or memory you can hold on to. This means that you will only focus on the present and your ego will not exist.

When you let go of your memories and focus only on the stillness, you will experience pure consciousness. When you are conscious, you only know the truth and it is difficult to describe the truth.

In this type of spiritual meditation, you focus on your subconscious. You will pay attention to your consciousness and learn the truth of who you are. When you practice this type of meditation, you will learn to let go of all your concerns since you withdraw your attention from the past and future. You will find yourself in the present and access reality.

Unifying Phrase Meditation

This type of meditation is a great way to shift your attention from your thoughts to the truth of being or reality anytime during the day. You can shift your attention whenever you need to, regardless of whether you are performing your daily tasks or sitting down.

It is important to remember that suffering only originates in your mind, and spiritual meditation will help you relax and pay attention to your consciousness. The phrases that you repeat in this type of meditation are not affirmation. These phrases will serve as a vehicle using which you can shift your attention from the suffering to your consciousness. Every word carries a vibration and can point towards the truth that lies within you. You should learn to pick the right phrases and only use those words that uplift you.

Yoga

This section covers some of the different types of meditation that are practiced in yoga. The third eye meditation is one of the most common meditation techniques.

Third Eye Meditation

In this type of meditation, you should focus on the spot or area between your eyebrows. This area is known as the third eye or the ajna chakra. You should direct your attention to this point. If you find that your mind is chasing a specific thought or emotion, redirect your mind to focus on the third eye. This helps to silence your mind.

Chakra Meditation

You should focus on one of the chakras in your body, preferably one of the major chakras, using a mantra or visualization. If you use a mantra, identify the word that is associated with the chakra and only say that word in your mind or aloud when you meditate. This type of meditation is done on the crown chakra, the third eye, and the heart chakra.

Trataka or Gazing Meditation

In this type of meditation, you fix your gaze on an external object. When you close your eyes, you should continue to visualize the same object in your mind. This type of meditation helps you to train both the visualization and concentration powers of your mind.

Kriya Yoga

Kriya yoga is a set of breathing, energizing, and meditation exercise. It was taught by Paramahansa Yogananda and is suited for those who seek the spiritual aspects of meditation. To perform this type of meditation, you must learn to be self-aware.

Nada Yoga or Sound Meditation

As the name suggests, this type of meditation focuses only on sound. When you begin the process, you must focus on external sounds such as classical or instrumental music. This will help to calm your mind. When you master the art of focusing only on external sound, you should learn to focus on the internal sound of your mind and body. The goal is to hear a sound without the vibration, called the "para nada." This sound manifests as "OM."

Tantra

Tantra practices are not about ritualized sex. This is a wrong notion that the West has about tantra. Tantra is a rich tradition with numerous contemplative practices. There are close to 110 meditations listed in the Vijnana Bhairava Tantra text, and some of them require you to exercise great control over your mind.

Pranayama

This exercise helps you regulate your breathing. It is not meditation, but is an excellent way to calm your mind and prepare yourself for meditation. There are many types of pranayama, and the simplest one is the "4-4-4-4." In this method, you should breathe in while counting to 4, then hold your breath for 4 seconds, exhale while counting to 4 and then hold for 4 seconds. You should breathe through the nose and ensure that it is your abdomen and not your chest that moves. You should go through a few cycles like this. When you regulate your breathing, you will learn to balance your mood and pacify your body.

Kundalini Yoga

This type of meditation is a physically active form that blends mantras and deep breathing with movements. People learn this type of meditation from a teacher or a class, although it is easy to learn these mantras and poses at home. Kundalini yoga is similar to other types of yoga and can reduce pain and improve physical strength. It can also improve your mental health by reducing depression and anxiety. Multiple studies conducted on kundalini yoga conclude that it helps to increase energy, reduce pain, and improve mental health.

To perform this type of meditation, follow the steps below:

Step 1:

The first step is to energize your breath. You can perform breathing exercises if you are emotionally drained or tired. When you perform this exercise, you have to feel energized. Sit down on the ground or on a chair and close your eyes. Place your hand by your side and take a deep breath. Fill your lungs with air and count to 5 before you exhale through your mouth. Continue to perform this exercise at least 5 times. Now, let your breathing return to its natural rhythm. When you feel more energetic, slowly open your eyes and give yourself a few minutes to reorient yourself.

Step 2:

Continue to sit down and place your palms in front of you with your fingers facing the ceiling.

Step 3:

Take a deep breath, and break your breath into 4 parts. This means that you should pause 4 times when you take a breath before you let the air reach your lungs. Once you have filled your lungs, exhale and break the breath into 4 parts. There is no pattern that you should follow. You should break your breath where you feel comfortable. Repeat this process 4 times.

Step 4:

You should pull in your belly button every time you inhale and exhale. When you break your breath into 4 parts, you should pull your belly button in 4 times. You should do the same when you exhale. Continue this activity for 1 or 2 minutes.

Step 5:

You can now introduce a mantra. Most people find it difficult to focus on their breath. If you are distracted, add the "Sa–Ta–Na–Ma" mantra. The mantra means "Infinity–Life–Death–Rebirth." This mantra can be said once when you inhale and once when you exhale. The syllables of the mantra coincide with each part of your breath. Since this is a breathing exercise, it is difficult to say the mantra aloud. Therefore, you can say the mantra in your head.

Step 6:

When you are ready to end the meditation process, inhale deeply and hold your hands in front of you. Press your palms together and hold the position for 15 seconds. This posture will make your body tense. Now, exhale with force and relax your hands. Repeat this process once more, and slowly open your eyes.

Sufi Meditation

Sufism is a path within Islam, which is esoteric. The goal of Sufism is to purify yourself from within and create a bond with the Supreme. People who practice Sufism are known as Sufis and they use many practices to develop this bond. Most of these practices were influenced by yoga. Some of their techniques include:

- Sufi mantra meditation
- Contemplation of God
- Sufi breathing meditation
- Five elements breathing
- Heartbeat meditation
- Gazing meditation
- Sufi whirling
- Sufi walking meditation
- Bond of love meditation

Transcendental Meditation

This is a spiritual type of meditation where the practitioner will remain seated on the ground or in a chair and breathe slowly. The objective is to rise above, or transcend, the current state of being. During the session, you should repeat a set of words or a mantra to maintain focus. You should meet with a teacher to learn your mantra since the teacher will determine the mantra based on some factors, including your birth year. An alternative method allows you to choose your mantra. This is a modern version of this type of meditation. You can repeat sentences like, "I know I can achieve my goals," when you meditate. People who practice this type of meditation regularly will be more mindful.

The Mantra

One of the important differences between other forms of meditation and transcendental meditation is the use of a mantra. In this type of meditation, you use a mantra as a way to settle your mind down. In the traditional transcendental meditation, the mantra is a meaningless sound while in the contemporary version of this meditation; the mantra can be a word, a phrase or a sentence.

Most meditation techniques focus on emptying your mind, but this type of meditation is about letting all of your thoughts come and go. This is an incredible strategy since it allows you to let go of all the stress and anxious thoughts that you have. You learn to create a space between your mind and your thoughts.

The Practice

If you want to practice transcendental meditation, you should approach a certified teacher and take some courses to understand the practice. When you gain enough experience, you can meditate twice a day for at least 30 minutes. Experts say that this type of meditation helps one relax. To perform this type of meditation, follow the steps given below:

- Wear comfortable clothing.

- Sit in a comfortable chair and place your feet on the ground. Place your palms in your lap, but do not cross them.

- Close your eyes. Inhale and exhale deeply for 10 seconds.

- Now, open your eyes and focus on a point in the room, and then close them again. You will not open your eyes until your session is complete.

- Use the mantra that your teacher gave you and repeat it in your mind. This mantra is a sanskrit sound.

- When your mind is distracted by a thought, repeat the mantra in your head. After 30 minutes, wiggle your toes and move your fingers to bring yourself back to this world.

- Open your eyes and stare at a point in the room.

- Sit down for a few minutes and allow your mind to reorient itself.

Guided Meditation

Guided meditation is a modern phenomenon and is an easy way to start meditating. There are many apps that you can download if you want to perform guided meditation. Most of the techniques used in guided meditation are a combination of the techniques mentioned above.

This practice of meditation requires you to have some willpower and be determined to follow the instructions you hear. In the past, people were committed to meditating since there were strong ideals that fueled that commitment. Life, then, was simpler and there were fewer distractions.

However, we live in a different era now and our life is certainly busier. Most people do not have the willpower to work on specific tasks. There are many distractions everywhere, and people use meditation when they want to improve themselves, enhance their performance or develop better mental health.

It is for these reasons that guided meditation is a good way to start meditating. When you get the hang of it and want to take it to the next level, use some of the techniques listed above without the audio. You should decide if you want to take this step or not.

You can equate guided meditation to cooking with a recipe. This is a good way to start, but you cannot expect to make all your food by following a recipe. When you understand the ingredients and flavors, you can start cooking your own dish. It will have a different taste, but it will taste better than the dish you prepared by following a recipe.

How to do it

Guided meditation always comes in the form of an audio or video file, and most of the techniques used will fall in one of the following categories:

Traditional Meditation: In this type of audio, the teacher only guides you. He or she will help you guide your attention to focus on your breath to ensure that you are in the meditative state. These audios often have no music and have more silence. Some examples are the guided meditation offered by Tara Brach and Thich Nhat Hanh. Their audios are rooted in the Buddhist practices and the purpose of these audios is to help the listener develop the practice and benefit from it.

Guided Imagery: These audios use the power of imagination and visualization. The teacher will guide you to imagine a scenery, journey, object or entity. The purpose behind this type of meditation is relaxation or healing.

Body Scans and Rrelaxation: The teacher will help you relax your whole body. The audios usually have nature sounds or soothing music. In yoga, this type of meditation is known as yoga nidra.

Affirmations: The teacher uses guided imagery and relaxation techniques to imprint any message in your mind. These affirmations are always positive.

Binaural Beats: Heinrich Wilhelm Dove discovered the Bbinaural Bbeats in 1839. When two frequencies are placed next to each ear, your brain will try to identify the difference between the two sounds.

Rafael Kain

Chapter Thirteen: How should You Come Out of Meditation?

You have worked on how you must sit and breathe. But how do you come out of meditation? Do you simply open your eyes, get up and leave? No. There is a three-step procedure that you must follow to ensure that you have meditated correctly.

Reflect on the Meditation

This step will help you better with your forthcoming meditation sessions. You must ask yourself questions about the entire session. You can ask yourself about the time when you felt completely at peace. If you have identified that, you can ask yourself which part of your body you were focusing on when you felt that way. In your next session, you can begin by focusing on that part of your body. If you cannot remember, it is all right. But the next session makes sure that you focus on these aspects. You must be the perfect salesperson. Only when you know what your customers like will you be able to sell your products! Meditation works in much the same way. You must know what your body wants before you move on to the next session.

Spread Goodwill and Cheer

After a session of meditation, you will feel happy about yourself and find a new sense of energy within yourself. You will have to spread this energy to other beings around you. These beings could be people around you or even plants. They are companions of any kind. You must hope to spread goodwill, cheer and hope for the wellbeing of the people around you.

Show Sensitivity to Your Breath Energy

You have shown sensitivity to your breath energy while you were meditating. Do not forget the breath energy after you have opened your eyes. There may be daunting tasks ahead of you. But make sure that you do not forget your breath energy. Make sure that you keep the breath energy flowing through you, irrespective of what the situation may be. Do not lose track of the energy due to the chores and duties that you must complete through the course of the day. This helps in keeping you grounded, which gives you a sense of security.

Chapter Fourteen: What is Mindfulness?

Have you ever walked into a room and realized that you do not remember why you walked in? Have you gone out for a run and reached a spot without realizing what route you took to get there? Well, most of us have. These are some examples of mindfulness, and is a state that people sometimes refer to as "autopilot."

When we slip into this mode, we do not live in the present since we are focusing on the thoughts running through our mind. Studies conclude that an average person is in this mode at least 47% of the time.

Some teachers say that a person in this mode is often dreaming since they are not present fully right now. In this busy world, it is easy for people to lose themselves in their thoughts for most of the day.

When we live this way, we forget to appreciate the beauty around us and fail to listen to what our bodies tell us. We stick to a mechanical way of living and forget that it can be harmful to us and for the people around us.

In autopilot mode, we often find ourselves lost in the process of doing something, so much so that we forget to live. We constantly struggle and strive to get our "stuff" done.

We will also be vulnerable to stress, depression, reactivity, and anxiety. Studies show that people are less happy when their minds wander.

What is Mindfulness?

Mindfulness is the opposite of autopilot mode. When you are mindful, you wake up and bring your attention back to the present. You can be mindful when you are constantly aware of your feelings, thoughts, the surrounding environment, and any sensations. Mindfulness also ensures that you pay attention to your feelings and thoughts like an impartial witness. This means that you should accept those thoughts and feelings without taking them too personally.

Jon Kabat-Zinn provided another definition of mindfulness: "Paying attention, on purpose, in the present moment, non-judgmentally."

People across the globe accept this definition since it helps people identify the exact components of mindfulness. This definition also helps one understand that their attention can shift in 3 ways when they practice mindfulness.

You Hold Your Attention on Purpose

Mindfulness ensures that you deliberately, and consciously, hold your attention. When you are on autopilot, your attention is swept up by never-ending thoughts. When you are mindful, you know you should wake up and ignore those thoughts. This gives you the ability to place your attention where you choose.

When I say, "you hold your attention on purpose," I mean that you are conscious of your thoughts. You learn to live more consciously and are fully aware of yourself and your surroundings when you pay attention in this way.

Your Attention is Immersed in the Present

If you allow the mind to do whatever it pleases, it will wander away from the current situation. Your mind always replays your memories, and projects those memories into the future. This means that people are often never fully present in the current moment.

When you are mindful, you are always engaged in the present moment and only focus on your experiences. You learn to let go of any tension you cause yourself by wanting things in your life to be different than what they are, and constantly wanting more from life. Instead, you learn to accept the current moment the way it is.

You do not Judge Your Thoughts

When you practice mindfulness, you do not aim to suppress or control your thoughts. You only want to focus on your experiences without labeling them or judging them. Through mindfulness, you learn to watch your thoughts, and emotions arise without worrying about them or being swept away by the force of that thought or emotion. When you learn to watch your thoughts and emotions you will not repeat your old ways of living and thinking. You learn to choose the way you want to live life.

How to Practice Mindfulness?

You can practice mindfulness in two ways. The first method is the formal practice, referred to as mindfulness meditation. This method is explained earlier in the book. In simple words, this practice requires you to sit down, close your eyes and focus on your breath. The second method is pretty much the rest of your life. When you perform any task in life and you are fully aware of what you are doing, you are being mindful. You can be mindful when you go for a walk, are washing the dishes or waiting in line for your coffee. You can transform any routine activity into a mindful activity when you pay attention to what you are doing. The last chapter of the book covers some mindfulness exercises that you can use to ensure that you are mindful every day in your life.

Benefits of Mindfulness

Due to the many studies conducted on mindfulness and the exposure from media, the world has become aware of what mindfulness is. This concept is no longer hidden in the monasteries, ashrams, and spiritual texts, and people all over the globe practice mindfulness. Students practice mindfulness since it helps them improve their exam performance. When people understand the benefits of mindfulness, they want to practice it to understand it better. Let us look at how mindfulness can help you:

Mindfulness helps to relieve a person of anxiety, depression, stress and other destructive emotions. When you practice mindfulness, the amygdala reduces in size, thereby reducing the sudden pumping of adrenaline in a stressful situation. The amygdala is responsible for your body's response to stress and, therefore, is the part of your brain that is responsible for destructive emotions like unhappiness, anger, and fear.

Multiple studies conclude that mindfulness helps to reduce depression, without any side effects. There would be no more need to take medication to avoid any negative thoughts, if you practice mindfulness regularly.

Mindfulness increases your physical and mental energy, reduces lethargy, increases your self-esteem and sense of wellbeing, and reduces insomnia.

Through mindfulness, one can learn to manage pain.

Mindfulness ensures that you are aware of your thoughts and emotions by making you pay attention to your thought processes. Therefore, it helps to increase attention and focus.

Mindfulness improves a person's social and emotional intelligence since it improves their compassion and empathy. It also helps to improve any relationship.

Mindfulness boosts immunity and improves health. Mindfulness is known to have beneficial effects on patients suffering from heart disease or terminal illnesses such as cancer.

You learn to think clearly and focus on the object or situation at hand, thereby improving your efficiency.

Mindfulness helps a person become more confident.

If you suffer from any addictions, mindfulness will help you focus on the present and not worry about your addiction. You can also practice mindfulness if you want to lose weight since studies show that it can work better than a diet.

Mindfulness also determines whether you will be happy in life or not.

Mindfulness can transform your whole world. If you have not already tried to be mindful, why not try it now and see what it is about? There are some exercises given in the last chapter of the book. When you use those exercises, you will discover a world that is full of surprises. You will learn that whatever you are searching for has always been inside you.

Chapter Fifteen: Debunking Myths about Mindfulness

People always worry about whether a new technique is good or not. Some of their questions often become myths, and people who read these myths believe that you do not need to practice mindfulness in order to be happy. This chapter debunks some of the myths of mindfulness.

You Should Only Focus on One Thing

People often believe that mindfulness is like meditation and breathing. The purpose behind mindfulness is to ensure that the mind focuses only on an object and not on the stray thoughts. This simple definition does not do justice to mindfulness. If you dig a little deeper, mindfulness is much more than just this.

The process of mindfulness comes from the Tibetan word drenpa, which means to retain, collect or remember. Therefore, it does not teach you how to observe your mind but teaches you to be conscious of your thoughts and every moment of your life. This improves the quality of your thoughts.

Mindfulness is all about concentrating on the present. If a tennis player should improve his or her backhand, they will practice the same shot for hours. Therefore, we should train our conscience to be more effective.

Mindfulness is Not Psychological Therapy

You cannot define mindfulness as a psychological therapy since this process cannot replace any psychological medicine or treatment. If you have a mental disorder, you should consult a medical professional and undergo the required treatment.

Concentration and relaxation exercises can complement medication and diagnosed treatment, but you cannot use them as a substitute. Therefore, it is wrong to assume that these exercises have therapeutic effects on the body. It is better to term these effects as regulatory since they only complement the medical treatments.

Empty Your Mind if You Want to Meditate

People believe that they should clear their mind before they practice any mindfulness exercise. It is important to remember that mindfulness does not require you to empty your mind. You must direct your mind and let it wander where it pleases. This means that you must master control over your thoughts and emotions. You must learn to guide your mind and not let any external stimuli guide it for you.

The human brain always thinks. It is because of this that it becomes hard for people to ward off any negative thoughts. When they try to ward off a negative thought, it comes back into their mind with a greater intensity than before. You should never block the thought, but let it flow.

Only if People are Relaxed can They be Mindful

People who practice mindfulness exercises are not relaxed. When they finish the exercises, they believe they have developed an internal sense of control and can take on any challenge. In fact, people who are restless gain more from a mindfulness exercise. This does not mean that mindfulness exercises keep you calm. These exercises will help you control your mind. This will help you be more grateful and appreciate every moment in life.

Positivity and Joy Come from You

It is important to remember that mindfulness is not synonymous with positivity or joy. It only helps you live in the present. When you perform a mindfulness exercise, you will not always have a smile on your face, because you accept your thoughts for what they are. You will learn to accept every thought and emotion, regardless of whether it is positive or not. Mindfulness will help you live every moment, good or bad, intensely. It enhances your experience and will help you channel your emotions and manage them better. You will stop judging your thoughts and actions, and learn to be more objective in your life.

Changing Your Habits

It is said that people can either start or change a habit in 21 days. Unfortunately, this is not how mindfulness works. You do not have to practice mindfulness every day of every week since the benefits of mindfulness are immediate.

You will notice the same benefits if you perform the exercise once a year or twice a day. All you need is willpower. You must also master the technique if you wish to reap the benefits faster. Mindfulness exercises are not about finding a quiet place to meditate.

It Takes Time

People cannot say they do not have the time to perform a mindfulness exercise. They always have the time, but they also have enough excuses. The problem here is that people take time to understand why they cannot or do not want to do it. All you need is 15 minutes and the desire to focus to perform these exercises. You can be cooking, walking, reading, etc. but you can still focus on what is happening right now. If you do it regularly, you will see that you are meditating without realizing that you are.

You Escape Reality

People believe that a meditation technique always tries to isolate them from the reality and ignore the worries of your life. This is untrue since you are trying to find the reason behind the stress. When you give your undivided attention, you will learn to observe the origin of stress and be conscious of it. You must make the effort to stop going away from reality. Instead, try to focus on the problem and see what you can do to solve it.

It is Boring

This is the most common myth about mindfulness. How can mindfulness be boring when there are so many ways to practice it? Do you believe that self-discovery is boring? People should probably talk about fear instead of boredom. Most people are worried about what they will discover if they look within themselves. The unknown and uncertain always terrifies us, and if it is something that has caused us pain in the past, we will do our best to ignore it. Remember that you can free yourself from those negative emotions.

Chapter Sixteen: Mindfulness Exercises

Generally, those who meditate are healthier, more successful, and happier than people who do not meditate. If the benefits of mindfulness and meditation make you want to practice mindfulness exercises, you have come to the right place. You may have tried both meditation and some mindfulness exercises in the past. When you could not control your thoughts, you decided that you have a mind that does not listen to reason and will never follow instructions. This is a belief that limits your potential. Mindfulness is a skill, and it will take practice. You must constantly perform mindfulness exercises to become an expert.

Remember that the only thing standing between you and your goal is direction. This chapter provides some of the best mindfulness exercises and guides you through each of these exercises. Some of these exercises are for groups, therefore, it is best if you find others who take mindfulness seriously, before you perform these exercises.

Mindfulness Activities for Group Therapy and Groups

In most cases, group therapies show promising results and they are as effective as cognitive behavioral therapy (CBT), which is a process that psychologists use to treat their patients. There is sufficient evidence that shows group mindfulness therapies are as effective as individual CBTs. Since there are many people suffering from clinical issues and there are not many clinical psychologists who can treat them, it is best to resort to individual treatments. You can attend group mindfulness sessions since they help you work on your stress, anxiety, and other health problems.

The Fleming and Kocovski Treatment Plan

Fleming and Kocovski devised a plan to treat a group of patients suffering from anxiety. The plan they used for the treatment is a great example of a mindfulness exercise. You can use this treatment plan if you are working with a group.

The exercises used in this treatment plan were effective

and treated patients suffering from social anxiety disorder. These exercises can also be applied to different groups and will still see positive results.

The treatment plan uses an eight-member group. This group should meet every week for 2 hours for a period of 12 weeks. The first part of every session will be devoted to a discussion and a mindfulness exercise.

The following is the list of mindfulness exercises conducted in every session:

1. Raisin exercise
2. Body scan
3. Mindful seeing
4. Mindfulness of the breath, sounds, and thoughts
5. Acceptance of thoughts and feelings exercise
6. Acceptance of social Anxiety
7. Mountain meditation
8. Breath focus without guidance
9. Lake meditation
10. Non-guided breath focus

This chapter covers some of the mindfulness exercises mentioned above. These exercises aim to reduce social anxiety disorder. Some of the exercises mentioned in this chapter can be used by groups and some can only be performed by an individual. Every exercise is described well and you will learn how to perform each of these exercises.

The Raisin Exercise

The raisin exercise is a great way for someone to practice mindfulness. Anyone can attempt this exercise using any type of food, although food with interesting and unusual textures is the perfect object to use in this exercise. Hold a raisin in your hand and pretend like you have never seen it before. Now, pay attention to the following:

- How the raisin feels in your hand
- How the raisin looks
- How the raisin reacts when you squeeze it
- How it smells
- And finally, how it tastes

When you focus on a single object, you will bring your

mind to the present and focus on what is in front of you. When you focus on what is in front of you, you will be mindful and will learn to be more aware of your surroundings. You will begin to focus on the present.

The Body Scan

The body scan is a popular exercise for people who practice mindfulness. This exercise does not require many tools or props and can be performed by beginners, too.

Let us look at the 30-minute body scan exercise that John Kabat-Zinn mentions in his mindfulness-based stress reduction techniques.

Step 1:

Lie on your back and keep your palms facing upward. You should place your legs slightly apart. You can also perform this exercise when you sit on a chair where your feet will rest on the ground.

Step 2:

You should lie very still for the rest of the exercise and only move with awareness. This means that you should only move when your mind believes that it is necessary.

Step 3:

You should first focus on your breath and notice the rhythm of it. Notice your experience when you inhale and exhale. You should not change the way you breathe, but only pay attention to how you are breathing.

Step 4:

You should then focus on how your clothing feels against your skin. Focus on how the floor feels when you lie down on it. See how the temperature of your body and environment change with your thoughts and emotions.

Step 5:

Now, pay attention to those parts of the body that are sore, feel heavy or light, or are tingling. You should make note of the parts of your body where you do not feel any sensations at all or are hypersensitive.

This exercise will run through every part of your body. You should pay attention to how every area of your body feels. The scan moves in the following way:

- The toes of both feet
- The rest of your feet starting from the top, bottom and then the ankles
- Lower legs

- Calves and knees
- Thighs
- Pelvic region (your buttocks, pelvic bone, tail bone, and your genitals)
- Then the abdomen
- Followed by the chest
- The lower back
- Upper back — back, ribs, and shoulder blades
- Arms (forearm, biceps, triceps, and elbows)
- Hands (palms, back, fingers, and wrists)
- Neck
- Face and head (your mouth, jaw, nose, ears, cheeks, eyes, scalp, forehead, top and back of the head)
- And finally, ending it with the blowhole. The blowhole is the imaginary hole that is at the top of your head. You should visualize that your breath is moving out of your body through the blowhole.

Once the body scan is complete, you can slowly open

your eyes and move to your natural sitting position. Make note of how you feel and the thoughts that are running through your mind.

Mindful Seeing

When there are no visual stimuli, you may find it difficult to see in your mind. Not everybody is able to use their imagination. This activity is helpful for those people who identify with this feeling. It is a simple exercise that requires a window with any view. To perform this exercise, follow the steps given below:

Step 1:

Find a space outside the window where there are some sights that you can observe.

Step 2:

Look at everything outside the window, and do not label or categorize what you see. Instead of identifying the object as a tree, bird or a sign, try to focus on the colors, textures, and patterns.

Step 3:

Pay attention to how the objects move because of the wind or any other factor. Notice the different shapes in the scene outside the window. You should look outside the window as if you are doing it for the first time. Try to look at these objects as if you are unfamiliar with them.

Step 4:

Observe the objects but do not criticize them. You should be aware of the object but not focus only on one object.

Step 5:

If you are distracted, you should rein your thoughts and notice the shapes and colors of the objects in front of you.

This exercise only lasts for a few minutes, but gives you the opportunity to discover a whole new world.

Mindful Listening

This activity is taken from the positive psychology kit where a group works on mindful listening. This is an important skill to develop and is a great mindfulness exercise for a group. People thrive and work well when they believe that they have been "seen" or "heard." In other words, this exercise helps you pay attention to the people around you and shift the focus from yourself to the people around you. Mindful listening helps to create an inner calm in both the speaker and the listener since the speaker knows that the listener does not judge him or her. The listener is fully attentive and listens to what the speaker is saying since there is no inner chatter.

This exercise involves the following steps:

Step 1:

Invite every participant in the group and ask them to think of one thing they are worried about and one thing they are looking forward to.

Step 2:

When every participant is aware of these points, they should share a story with the rest of the group.

Step 3:

The speaker should pay attention to how they feel when they speak, how they feel when they address an issue they have hidden for so long, and how they feel when they share something positive.

Step 4:

When the participants have finished sharing their stories, the group can split into smaller groups and answer the questions below. You must then regroup and discuss the answers.

The questions every participant should ask are:

- What were your thoughts and emotions when you were speaking during the exercise?
- What were your thoughts and emotions when you were listening during the exercise?
- Did your mind wander?
- If yes, what were you thinking about?
- How did you bring your attention back to the present?
- Were you judging any speaker?
- If yes, how did you feel when you judged them?
- Did you empathize with any speaker?
- If yes, how did you feel then?
- How did you feel right before you had to start speaking?
- How did you feel immediately after speaking?
- What thoughts are running through your head now?

- How would you feel if you practiced mindful listening with every individual you spoke to?

- Do you think this habit will change the way you listen to, interact with, and relate to the speaker?

- How would you feel if you always set the intention that you will pay attention to someone with kindness, curiosity, and acceptance?

- How would you feel if you projected that intention towards yourself?

In addition to these activities, the group can also choose to perform yoga, where they must maintain posture, focus on their breath, and be aware of their emotions and thoughts.

6 Fun Mindfulness Interventions, Techniques, and Worksheets for Adults

You can engage in mindfulness in multiple ways using worksheets, different exercises and techniques. If you find it difficult to participate in a group activity, you can perform these individual exercises.

The Self-Compassion Pause

You can always download a worksheet on the self-compassion pause since it will guide you through the exercise. You will learn to be compassionate towards yourself and also be mindful. This is an ideal exercise for people who need to show themselves compassion, especially when they know how to show compassion towards others. It is also a great way to practice mindfulness since you become aware of your emotions and stay in the moment.

- You must note the date and time on the worksheet and also make note of the primary object you want to focus on.

- Read the description provided in the worksheet and understand why it is important that you are compassionate towards yourself.

- To begin the exercise, sit down comfortably and close your eyes. Pay attention to your feelings by pausing your thoughts and actions. This will ensure that you are mindful of your emotions.

- You can give yourself a hug, place your hand over your stomach or heart, or make contact with yourself in some way. Then, take a few deep breaths.

- The final step is to acknowledge suffering. This step allows you to practice mindfulness and also encourages you to be mindful about your thoughts and emotions. The aim is to prevent yourself from being overwhelmed by the emotion or the pain. Instead, you should acknowledge it and give yourself the permission to feel the pain.

This last step is very difficult, but is an important step to complete. You will need to vocalize the following statements:

- This is pain or suffering.

- It is all right to feel pain and suffering since it is a part of being a human being.

- Think of a phrase that will allow you to offer compassion to yourself.

Self-Inquiry Meditation

This type of meditation focuses on self-inquiry and is used by people to enlighten themselves. This process begins in the same way as the previous exercise, where you should jot down the date and what area you choose to focus on today. You can download worksheets from the internet and go through the description of this type of meditation. Through self-inquiry, you will find peace and will be open to new experiences. Follow these steps to begin the exercise:

- Sit down in a comfortable position.

- Settle into your mind and body and clear your mind of your usual thoughts.

- Try to remove any negative thoughts from your mind.

- Focus on how it feels to be you. Ask yourself who you are and what your core beliefs and values are.

If you start to chase a specific thought or emotion, you should bring yourself back and ask yourself the following question, "Who is this thought occurring to?"

You can continue this exercise for as long as you want. This is a difficult exercise since you must focus on yourself, something that many don't find enjoyable. If you find it difficult to stay in your head, you should try to practice the self-compassion exercise first since the experience will make you feel better about yourself.

The objective of this exercise is to ensure that you are aware of yourself and aware of the beliefs that make you who you are. It is easy for people to be lost in their usual tasks and distractions. You will learn to be aware of the fact that you are dealing with these emotions and feelings.

The 5 Senses Exercise

This exercise, called "five senses," helps a person practice mindfulness in any situation they find themselves in. All they need to do is notice that they are experiencing a specific thought or emotion using these 5 senses. You must follow the order mentioned below.

Observe 5 things you can see

You should look around and bring your attention to 5 objects or things that you see. You should pick objects that you don't normally notice, like a small crack in the wall or the shadow of a tree.

Notice 4 things you feel

Focus on 4 things you feel right now, maybe the wind in your hair, the texture of your clothing, the surface of the table, etc. These feelings do not have to only be emotions.

Notice 3 things you hear

You should take a moment to listen and identify 3 things you can hear in the background. This can be the hum of a refrigerator, birds chirping, the wind, traffic, etc.

Notice 2 things you smell

You must bring your awareness to the smells that you often ignore, regardless of whether they are pleasant or not. For example, you might smell the pine trees because of the breeze, or smell the food from a restaurant nearby.

Notice 1 thing you taste

You should focus on 1 thing you can taste this very moment. You can chew a piece of gum, drink some water or eat something. Alternatively, you can simply open your mouth and taste the air.

This is an easy and quick exercise that you can perform which will help you be mindful of your surroundings. If you have only a few minutes to spare or don't have the tools to perform a body scan, you can use this exercise to bring awareness to the current moment, quickly.

The Mini-Mindfulness Exercise

If you don't have enough time to perform a mindfulness

exercise, then you can perform this exercise, since there are only 3 steps that you need to complete:

Step 1:

Move out of autopilot mode and be aware of what you are thinking, sensing, and doing, at that very moment. Sit down or stand in a comfortable posture, and notice your thoughts and emotions. Do not avoid them, but acknowledge them and let them pass. You must attune yourself to your current state.

Step 2:

You must then shift your awareness to your breathing for 1 minute. Count from 1 to 6 when you take a breath. The objective is to focus only on one thing. You must be aware of how your body moves when you take a breath, watch your chest rise and fall and how your belly moves in and out. Identify a pattern in your breath and anchor yourself to that pattern to live in the present.

Step 3:

Expand your awareness to the body and then to your surroundings. You should focus on the sensations you experience such as aches, tightness or maybe a light shining on your face. Always keep your mind whole and use it like a vessel for your inner self.

You can expand your awareness to the environment around you if you want to. You can focus on the objects in front of you, their shapes, patterns, colors, and textures. You should be present in this moment and be aware of your surroundings. When you want to finish the exercise, slowly open your eyes and carry that mindfulness with you throughout the day.

Walking Down the Street and Being Mindful

Your ability to observe your thoughts, sensations and emotions without trying to hide, solve or avoid them, is enhanced when you practice mindfulness exercises. When you are aware, you will learn to choose between actions and impulses that will help you learn to cope with your surroundings.

In the first step, you should visualize a scenario where you are walking down a familiar street. You constantly look down, but you feel that there is someone familiar on the other side of the street. You then look up at the person and wave. This person does not respond and walks by without looking back at you.

In the second step of this exercise, you should ask yourself the following questions. People find it difficult to differentiate between emotions and thoughts, since they play off each other rapidly. Ask yourself, What were my thoughts in that instance?

What did I feel when the person did not wave back at me?

In the last step, you should reflect on the series of thoughts and emotions that flooded your mind when your acquaintance behaved that way. You should then see if the exercise helped you see the situation differently and control your emotions.

Mindful Appreciation

In this exercise, you should notice 5 activities that you perform regularly but do not appreciate. Alternatively, you can also appreciate 5 objects or people who you see regularly but never appreciate. It all depends on you. Through this exercise, you will learn to appreciate and give thanks to things that you believe are insignificant. You will also learn to identify the things that support your existence, but you rarely think about them because you desire for better and bigger things. Take a notepad and write down 5 things that you think are insignificant, and check them off at the end of the day.

For instance, the postman comes to your house and delivers your mail, the clothes you wear keep you warm, the electricity powers the kettle and other kitchen appliances, you hear the birds chirping when you are at the bus stop, but:

- Do you know how these processes came into existence?

- Do you know how they work?

- Have you acknowledged or understood how these activities benefit you and the people around you?

- Do you ever think about life without these things?

- Do you stop and observe the intricate and finer details?

- Have you sat down and identified the relationship between these objects and how they are interconnected?

- Do you know how the relationship between these objects plays a role in the functioning of the earth?

When you identify 5 things and have written them down

in your notepad, you should do your best to understand the purpose of those objects. You should then learn to appreciate them because they support your life.

Mindful Awareness

The mindful awareness exercise enhances your appreciation and awareness of daily tasks and the results that you achieve. Think of an action that you perform regularly, like opening a door or a window. This is an action that you take for granted. When you touch the doorknob or the lock on the window, pay attention to how you feel and be mindful of your surroundings. Understand your feelings and emotions, and see where the door or window leads you.

You can perform the same exercise when you switch your computer on at work. You should take a moment to appreciate your brain because it understands how the system works. You should also appreciate your hands since they know which button they need to press.

These cues do not have to always be physical. For example, when you think of a negative thought, you can choose to stop that thought. You can label it as an unhealthy thought and release the negativity. Alternatively, when you smell food, you should take a moment to appreciate your good fortune because you have food to eat.

You should always choose a touch point that resonates with you now, and stop doing your chores in autopilot mode. You should take a few moments to develop awareness of where you are and what you are doing.

Walking Meditation

If you go for a run or walk in the morning, for at least 20 minutes, you can perform this exercise. You should perform this exercise in an area where you do not have too may distractions. Alternatively, you can try it anywhere and compare your results.

Like every other mindfulness activity, this exercise is also about paying attention to objects that are not your thoughts or emotions. You can concentrate on the sensations you feel when your feet touch the ground. You can also focus on your breath and focus on how different parts of your body react when you breathe. The objective is to develop a sort of attention that is relaxed. If you find that your mind is chasing a thought, bring it back without berating yourself.

If you are walking in the park or in an area with

greenery, you should increase the length of your session. Try to be more aware of the nature around you. You can observe the different objects around you and focus on them. You can listen to the birds calling, the rumble of traffic, the wind and the sun warming your face. Your mind will wander and focus on a thought. Shift your attention back to your surroundings and appreciate nature. People perform this exercise when they are in nature, but do not label it as a mindfulness exercise. Regardless of what you call it, your attention is only on the present and that is what matters most.

The 3 Minute Breathing Space

Unlike the body scan or meditation, this exercise is easy to perform and it does not take too long. If you lead a busy life, you can practice this exercise when you have 3 minutes to spare. With body scans and meditation, thoughts often creep into your head and it becomes difficult for a person to keep a clear and quiet head.

This is a technique that any individual can use since it only takes 3 minutes to perform. The exercise can be divided into the following sections and you should spend 1 minute on each of them:

- Spend the first minute answering a question on how you are doing in that very moment. Focus on the thoughts, sensations, and feelings that run through your mind when you ask yourself this question and try to label these feelings using words.

- Spend the next minute keeping yourself aware of your breath. Observe what happens to your abdomen when you take a breath.

- Use the last minute to expand your awareness. Instead of focusing only on your breath, try to feel how the breath flows through your nostrils and through your body.

This exercise is challenging since thoughts will creep into your mind. Instead of avoiding these thoughts, let them come into your mind. Do not pay too much attention to them. They will eventually disappear again. Remember to only observe your thoughts.

Every exercise that is mentioned in this section of the chapter will benefit an individual or a group of people. These exercises are often beneficial to client groups, but some of these exercises are better than the others since there are fewer errors that one encounters.

You must remember that mindfulness exercises help to

train your mind, and it will take some time before you can see the benefits of these exercises. Your mind will take some time to think differently, and the trick is to persevere. You should approach the process with some compassion and give yourself the time to reflect. Remember that you can shift from one exercise to the other depending on whether it works for you or not.

Introducing Dialectical Behavioral Therapy (DBT)

DBT is a cognitive behavioral therapy that is often used to treat patients with borderline personality disorder.

- The first step is to identify some behaviors that are life threatening. People with severe mental illnesses often display these behaviors.

- The therapist must identify the behaviors or reactions that interfere with therapy. Skipping sessions, unable to control anger, and refusal to meet the goals of the therapy are some of the behaviors that create an obstacle between treatment and the patient or client.

- Finally, the therapist will identify the behaviors that affect the patient's quality of life, and look for ways to correct those behaviors. These include bad financial decision-making, problems with communication, and non-productive behaviors.

Any behavioral skills taught in individual or group therapy fall into the following categories:

- Distress tolerance
- Mindfulness
- Emotional regulation
- Interpersonal effectiveness

A therapist ensures that his or her client is always mindful and aware of his or her thoughts and feelings, and this is the core skill that is taught in DBT. When a client practices mindfulness, they learn to control the pace of their thoughts, understand their thoughts and sharpen their awareness and focus.

The Effectiveness of DBT – Mindfulness - Dialectical Behavior Therapy

A study included DBT mindfulness training alongside regular psychiatric treatment to test the effectiveness. Modules were developed on mindfulness to help every patient achieve a mind that is aware of every thought and emotion. These modules focused on the "what" and "how" skills.

The "What" Skills

These set of skills help a client learn how to:

- Observe and be aware of their experience.

- Describe that experience using labels

- Be present fully in a moment and in their thoughts and actions, without being conscious

These skills help clients to become aware of everything that is happening to them and what role they play in their experience. When you become aware of your thoughts, you stay grounded in the present. This creates the foundation for the "how" skills.

The "How" Skills

The "how" skills refer to the process of teaching a patient to observe, describe, and be a part of his or her experience. These skills help the client:

- Learn to not pass judgment, regardless of what their experience is

- Focus only on one thought or experience at a time and learn to control their attention if it begins to wander

- Focus on their goals and work towards those goals, regardless of how they feel

The clients also went through a series of interventions

where the focus was mindfulness. These clients were subject to exercises such as the body scan, mindful breathing and other awareness exercises and practices. The outcome of this study showed that an individual who received this training, along with the usual treatment, showed better results when compared to the group that only received the traditional treatment. It was also found that when an individual spent more time on mindfulness exercises, they showed greater improvement.

DBT has taught the therapists and patients a wide range of exercises and techniques that will help an individual be mindful. The best news is that these exercises have different effects on people, but they will always ensure that the individual or group using these techniques will learn to be mindful.

5 Simple Mindfulness Exercises from DBT

There are many mindfulness exercises and techniques that are shared online, in addition to the mindfulness techniques that are used in clinical research. One source is the website DrivingPeace.com. This website offers its viewers some DBT-based techniques that help with anxiety. These techniques can also be used by those who don't suffer from anxiety. These exercises are easy and quick, therefore, you can practice them every day.

Observe a Leaf for 5 Minutes

All you need to do is pick up a leaf from the ground and place it in the palm of your hand. Now, pay attention to only that leaf for 5 minutes. You should notice the texture, color, pattern, and shape of the leaf. When you do this, your mind will realign itself to the present and align all your thoughts with your experience.

Eat Mindfully for 4 Minutes

This exercise is like the raisin exercise described above. If you are holding your food, focus on how that food feels in your hands. When you notice the texture, color, weight, etc. of the food, you can focus on the smell of the food. You can then focus on eating the food, but pay attention to how you are eating your food. You should notice the texture of the food against your tongue and how it tastes. This exercise will help you create new experiences with familiar food.

Observe Your Thoughts for 15 Minutes

This is the core of any mindfulness exercise, where you must be aware of your thoughts. This exercise enhances your awareness and helps you identify your thoughts immediately.

Lie down or sit down in a comfortable position and let the tension dissipate from your body. First, focus on your breathing and then move your attention to your body. Once you understand what it feels like to be in your body, move on to understanding and being aware of your thoughts.

You must always be aware of what thoughts, emotions, and feelings enter your mind. Do not judge or label these thoughts. As mentioned earlier, you should think about these thoughts as clouds in the sky. If you begin to chase a specific thought, learn to acknowledge that thought and gently move your attention back to your thoughts.

Mindfulness Bell Exercise for 5 Minutes

Begin this exercise by closing your eyes and listening. When you hear the signal, you should focus on the sound and continue to pay attention to that sound until it fades away. This will help to keep you grounded in the present. There are many sounds that you can use for this exercise, and you can find them all online.

Stare at the Center

Your objective is simple: choose a video where the pattern changes and only focus on the center of that pattern. Allow your mind to wander and notice every thought that comes into your mind, but ensure that you stay in the present.

This exercise is like the phenomenon of fixation, which is a result of staring at a campfire or a candle flame. You can bring the same deep thought and focus to this exercise, but ensure that you do not lose yourself in your thoughts. You must let your thoughts pass by and ensure that you stay in the present moment. You must use a video to practice this exercise.

Conclusion

Thank you once again for purchasing this book.

This book reveals a set of powerful and simple practices that you can follow in order to break the cycle of stress, unhappiness, and anxiety. The included exercises promote happiness and will allow you to meet every thought and emotion you feel with renewed courage.

Mindfulness allows you to be aware of every emotion or thought in your body and will help you use that awareness to lead a happy life. When you invest a few minutes each day in the exercises given in this book, you will gain control over your life. You must remember that you will not be mindful when you perform the exercise just once. It takes time and it is important to perform these exercises regularly to ensure that you are mindful in every aspect of your life. If you find that your mind is wandering when you are performing an exercise, do not berate yourself. Instead, bring your attention back to the present and focus on your breath.

I hope the information in this book has helped you understand what mindfulness is and I wish you luck on your journey.

Sources

https://exploringyourmind.com/8-myths-about-mindfulness/

https://liveanddare.com/types-of-meditation

https://positivepsychologyprogram.com/mindfulness-exercises-techniques-activities/

https://www.healthline.com/nutrition/12-benefits-of-meditation#section10

https://www.healthline.com/health/mental-health/types-of-meditation

https://www.lifehack.org/763013/types-of-meditation-techniques

https://www.artofliving.org/in-en/meditation/meditation-for-you/10-myths-meditation

https://www.pocketmindfulness.com/6-mindfulness-exercises-you-can-try-today/

https://renewyourmind.co.nz/introduction-mindfulness/

https://www.mindful.org/meditation/mindfulness-getting-started/

https://www.umassmed.edu/cfm/mindfulness-in-medicine/intro-to-mindfulness/

https://noetic.org/meditation-bibliography/intro-meditation

https://www.theguardian.com/lifeandstyle/2011/jan/22/how-to-meditate-mark-vernon

https://www.primermagazine.com/2015/live/a-modern-mans-introduction-to-meditation

https://www.helpguide.org/articles/stress/stress-symptoms-signs-and-causes.htm

https://www.healthline.com/health/stress

https://www.medicalnewstoday.com/articles/145855.php

http://www.stress.org.uk/what-is-stress/

https://www.webmd.com/balance/stress-management/stress-symptoms-effects_of-stress-on-the-body

https://www.stress.org/stress-effects/

https://www.healthline.com/health/whats-your-stress-type

https://spacioustherapy.com/3-types-stress-health-hazards/

https://www.psychologytoday.com/us/blog/turning-straw-gold/201406/7-myths-about-mindfulness

https://www.huffpost.com/entry/myths-about-mindfulness-to-stop-believing_b_8958372

https://exploringyourmind.com/8-myths-about-mindfulness/

www.ingramcontent.com/pod-product-compliance
Lightning Source LLC
Chambersburg PA
CBHW070102080526
44586CB00013B/1160